STRESSED IS DESSERTS SPELLED BACKWARD

Other Books by Brian Luke Seaward

Stand Like Mountain, Flow Like Water:
Reflections on Stress and Human Spirituality

Table For Two, Please:
Morals of Inspiration and Wisdom
Over the Noon Hour

Health and Wellness Journal Workbook

Managing Stress:
Principles and Strategies for
Health and Wellbeing

Managing Stress: A Creative Journal

STRESSED IS DESSERTS SPELLED BACKWARD

Rising Above Life's Challenges with Humor, Hope, and Courage

BRIAN LUKE SEAWARD, Ph.D.

Foreword by Joan Lunden

BARNES & NOBLE BOOKS
NEW YORK

This edition published by Barnes & Noble, Inc.,
by arrangement with Conari Press.

2000 Barnes & Noble Books

ISBN 0-7607-2386-9

Printed and bound in the United States of America

02 03 MC 9 8 7 6 5 4 3

BVG

For my Godparents,

Pat and Caleb O'Connor

STRESSED IS DESSERTS
SPELLED BACKWARD

STRESSED IS DESSERTS SPELLED BACKWARD

Foreword

Growing up, I always thought that what happened in my life would bring me happiness or cause me stress. One of the most important lessons I've learned is that it's not what happens to us, but our reaction to what happens to us that causes us stress. And that means we have the power to control our level of stress. We, in fact, have the power to choose not to react at all to that which happens around us.

It is not what life brings to us that determines our level of happiness and self-fulfillment. It is the attitude we bring to life. The most important decision we can make each day is our choice of attitude. It is what will spur us on or stand in our way. Since we are in charge of our attitude, we are the architects of our lives.

In this complex, uncertain, and always changing world, it is easy to lose sight of our power to achieve happiness and fulfillment and let the everyday pressures weigh us down. To best reach fulfillment without giving into the pressures, we all need encouragement and guidance along the way.

Brian Luke Seaward provides us with much needed hope, faith, strength, and direction in his masterful telling of stories that expand our vision and inspire us. Rather than telling us what to do or how we should be, he teaches by example. His stories encourage us to think about life and its stresses with a fresh point of view. They help us approach life's twists and turns with anticipation rather than fear. Luke Seaward shows us that while we cannot escape stress, there are many ways to deal with it effectively. His words have touched my life profoundly and helped me to find the grace and dignity, the patience and compassion, needed to navigate my ever-changing course. They have helped me understand that it is the way I choose to see the world that will create the world I see.

—Joan Lunden

section one

Dessert and Coffee— Make That Decaf! From Crumbs to Crêpes

"I'm an old man and I have known a great many problems in my life, most of which never happened."

—*Mark Twain*

THE RADIO HOST HAD JUST INTRODUCED ME to her listeners. At her request, I then made a few comments about the nature of stress and various ways in which to effectively deal with the pressures of life. It was 2:00 P.M. in Colorado, where I was seated in my living room. It was 4:00 P.M. in Washington, D.C. at her radio station. This was the "Voice of America," and the show was being broadcast live all around the world. "Sebastian from Paris, go ahead," she said. "Oui! Merci. Thanks for taking my call. My mother has cancer and I was wondering how best to deal with this?" I gave a short bit of advice which pleased him and we were on to the next call. For the next hour, people from all over the world called in on a toll-free line. There was Kim from Tokyo, Marion from Johannesburg, South Africa; Terif rang from Cairo. There was Sarah in London, Monica in São Paulo, Mohammed from Sri Lanka, Chee from Kuala Lumpur. Rajesh, from New Delhi, was the last call. For the entire hour, I was connected to the heartbeat of the planet. The World Health Organization calls stress "a global epidemic," and while I have quoted the WHO several times over the past few years, it was not until that afternoon in 1997 that I realized how true this fact was. Stress may be as American as apple pie, but it is also as worldwide as bread pudding. It doesn't matter who you are, where you live, how much money you make, or how dysfunctional your parents were while you were growing up—stress is a stranger to no one. For better or worse, stress is an inevitable fact of life. A theme common to stress is that of loss, whether the loss of a spouse, child, job, or life itself. While there is no escaping stress, there are many ways to deal with it effectively, which I hope you will discover as you make your way through this book. In a world filled with so much stress, surely there must be some good from it. Ageless wisdom tells us as much with metaphors that have become household clichés—from silver linings and lemonade to lessons, blessings, and gifts. In the midst of chaos and catastrophe, at first it may be difficult to see the silver lining or taste the lemonade. Even so, we must remind ourselves that there is a reason for every circumstance, even if we never become aware of it or, perhaps more likely, we don't agree with the reason when we do get a chance to glimpse the bigger picture. The bigger picture can often be clearly viewed from the vantage point of stories. Since the dawn of humanity, stories have been shared as a teaching tool, to guide souls further along the human path, sometimes as advice, but more often than not as a reminder of what we already know at a deeper level—that there is no separation from our divine source. Psychologists on the vanguard of conscious thought tell us that stories speak to the audience of perceptions housed in the right hemisphere of the brain. Stories penetrate and nurture those cognitive functions which are receptive to thought, open to ideas, impressionable to stimulus, and sympathetic to emotions. Nowhere is this better understood than through the recounting of fables, folklore, and fairy tales, each built on the foundation of a moral or human truth. Parables were the preferred method of teaching for Jesus of Nazareth, after all. It seems fitting, therefore, for me to structure this book, in the tradition of fables and fairy tales, around a series of stories which each end with a "moral," a nugget of truth that can be digested as a spiritual nutrient to feed the soul. Today, in the age of high technology and rushed lifestyles, stories are proving to be extremely popular in bringing the focus of life back to a soul level rather than operating at the unstable apex of ego. Theories and facts speak to the rational, linear mind; stories address issues of the heart and matters of the soul. In truth, both allegory and fact are needed to walk the human journey in balance. So let us begin with a story. Running up a flight of stairs with a glass milk bottle is not the smartest thing to do, but teenagers do foolish things. At thirteen, I had a habit of teasing the winds of fate, but the winds were particularly strong-willed on this day. Unsure footing prompted a sudden fall and shards of milk-covered glass became airborne like a hundred arrows released simultaneously from an enormous bow. One became embedded deep in my left hand. Blood soon pooled with milk, and a river of pink fluid cascaded down the wooden steps away from the kitchen. Sitting anxiously in the post-op recovery room with my mom, my left hand bandaged with several inches of gauze, I learned that, as bad as the accident was, it might have been much worse. The nerve that allows the hand muscles to contract was nearly severed. A fraction of a millimeter closer and my hand would have been paralyzed for life. The outcome still uncertain, I prayed with confidence. While my mom left the room to call my dad with the news, I turned to strike up a conversation with the young man who lay on a gurney beside me. Aside from a bandaged head, I noticed that his right hand and arm were atrophied. He had cerebral palsy. Learning of my accident, he assured me that I'd be fine. Before the nurse came in to wheel me to my room, he winked at me, made an eloquent reference to "spiritual muscles" (what some call inner resources), as he told me a joke, and then explained that exercising my funnybone would help me heal more quickly. I simply smiled back at him. But the lesson stuck, and sure enough, laughter and optimism not only helped heal my hand but many other difficult situations looming on the horizon. A year later, I learned firsthand that spiritual muscles include more than just humor and optimism. Riding home from church early one winter morning, our car was hit head-on by a truck that had skidded on ice and snow into our lane. My father and two sisters lay unconscious, bleeding, perhaps dead.

Shaken but uninjured, I ran for what seemed like miles in knee-deep snow to the nearest house to call the police and ambulance. With each breath of cool air, I found myself drawing upon the inner strength of courage and faith. Later that day, in a tense hospital waiting room, perhaps by coincidence, I spotted a man with cerebral palsy walking toward the emergency room. Once again I reflected on these spiritual muscles, as I prayed for the lives of my family. Humor, patience, compassion, courage, curiosity, humbleness, forgiveness, faith, creativity, persistence, confidence, and love comprise a short list of the divine inner resources that are our best medicine for tough times. The muscles of the soul are the tools we use to help dismantle and remove the roadblocks of life. I know firsthand that these muscles transcend the obstacles we call stress. Growing up under the roof of two alcoholic parents, I exercised my spiritual muscles (particularly faith and humor) regularly. I know they work! Like our physical muscles, these spiritual muscles need to be flexed, stretched, and moved against some form of resistance quite regularly to remain effective when confronting the problems we all encounter on the human journey. Ignored, they will never disappear completely but will certainly atrophy with disuse. Experts in the field of stress management don't necessarily concur on what stress is exactly. It's a rather complex subject. One thing they do agree on is that, by and large, stress is a perception, an interpretation of an event or circumstance which ultimately is understood to be a threat. Perceptions, most likely produced by the ego, sound the stress alarm and we quickly move into a "fight-or-flight" survival mode. While the stress response—the dynamics of human physiology that shunt blood to the arms and legs, increase breathing, and increase metabolism to do one thing: move—may be ideal for threats of a physical nature, this response is totally inappropriate for all other kinds of stress. Most of the threats we have today are not physical but mental, emotional, or spiritual. I venture to say that about 90 percent of perceived threats are of a spiritual nature, involving relationships, values, and purpose in life. This is all the more reason we need to exercise our soul-muscles to deal with the big and small challenges we encounter in life. As a child, I sought refuge from the dissonance that alcoholic dysfunction can bring to a family. I found solace in two places: the wooded forest behind my house, where I went when I felt the need to be alone; and my grandmother's kitchen for those times I needed a trusting smile and a hug. My grandmother was small in stature but mighty in character. Well versed in Washington, D.C.'s high society, extremely well educated, and quite savvy with regard to life's complexities, she was sharp as an owl and as graceful as a hummingbird, particularly when it came to the use of the English language. She too, had encountered her share of stressors in life: the Depression, several miscarriages, the premature death of her husband, and immobilization due to two broken hips. Although a private person by nature, my grandmother would openly recount her stories to me—with a little prodding. Through it all, she sailed through life quite gracefully. Anytime she saw a hint of distress in my eyes, she was quick to prepare me a plate of pastries and a glass of milk, saying, "Remember, honey: Stressed is desserts spelled backward." Following in her footsteps as a teacher, I have met scores of people—students, workshop participants, and complete strangers—

whom I think of as everyday heroes; people who, by the grace of God, emerge from what can only be described as a trip to hell with dignity and aplomb. Their experiences, many of which are recounted in this book, are testimonials to the use of inner resources and the remarkable human potential to deal with life's challenges in a way that promotes spiritual growth. Tiramisu, Crème Brûlée, and New York Style Cheesecake may be the most popular desserts these days, but it's obvious to me that humor, patience, and faith are the ingredients we need to transform any curse into a blessing. It is my wish that this collection of stories serves as a reminder of what we already know—that indeed, we are always in the presence of the divine. As we exercise and flex our spiritual muscles, we kiss the face of God. In an age of victimization, where whining about our problems has become the national pastime and calling a lawyer is the automatic reaction to an impending disaster, it is refreshing to note that there is an option: to let go of stress and move on gracefully, rather than play the recurring role of victim. More times than not, we can have our cake and eat it, too. And each time, the taste of dessert, after a long hard haul on the road of life, is sweet indeed.

section two

On a Wing and a Prayer

"HELP!" THIS WORD MIGHT NOT SOUND like a typical prayer, but it most certainly qualifies. No matter what mess we find ourselves in, lifting our eyes and voice to the heavens is the most common response, even among those who don't believe in God. It may stand to reason that the bigger the problem, the more intense the call for divine assistance, but the use of prayer as a coping technique is ubiquitous in every culture for all situations.

Moments of intense stress may lead us to believe that we have been divinely abandoned (if not punished), but those same moments of chaos may eventually bring upon us the realization that help is only a prayer away. Prayers, in all their many forms, are a call to faith—a belief or an intuitive knowing that we are part of something bigger, bigger than words can ever describe. Faith asserts that this bigger "something" (call it God, Allah, the Great Mystery, the Tao, or the big Kahuna) throws us a metaphorical lifeline—and at some point, we will catch it and be pulled in. A prayer answered is like a big hug.

There is no one way to pray. Faith, in the form of prayer, varies as greatly as those who take the leap. All prayers offered in sincerity, however, are equal to the ears of divine consciousness. Remember, patience is a silent partner in prayer as we put forth the clarion call to summon God's attention. All prayers are answered, but in God's time, not ours. That's where the wings come in—when we take the leap.

Faith is quite a personal undertaking. Scientists cannot measure it. Theologians cannot quantify it. Yet to those who employ it, faith is very real indeed. The following stories are examples of faith; the realization that no matter what the situation, we are never alone.

1

A Car Ride in Chicago

A business trip took me to the Windy City last summer. I had frequented Chicago many times during my graduate school days at the University of Illinois, Champaign-Urbana. I even ran the Chicago Marathon along Lake Shore Drive in what had to be one of the hottest days on record for the month of October. Aside from several layovers at O'Hare International Airport, however, this was my first trip back to the city in nearly twenty years.

I suppose I could have walked the three miles from my hotel down Michigan Avenue to meet a college friend for dinner, but in my tardiness I decided to take a cab. The bellman blew a whistle, and moments later wheels screeched as the yellow Checker pulled up to the entrance. The bellman opened the car door and I was off.

I find cab drivers to be an interesting group of people. It doesn't take a Ph.D. to drive a taxi, but more often than not the cab drivers I've encountered in big cities are a very well-educated bunch. For most, I've discovered, their first job on these shores is driving a cab until something better opens up. Some are between jobs, trying to make ends meet. By and large, cabbies are an honest group of citizens. This cab driver proved to be no different.

"Hi," I said, looking at his taxi license on the visor. Next to his photo was a picture of the Virgin Mary. A good sign, I thought.

"Hello," he replied with a thick European accent. "My name is Andreí."

Not placing his accent, I inquired where he was from.

"Poland. But I have lived here for several years. What brings you to my city?" he said, staring at me in the rearview mirror.

"I'm here at a conference giving a talk on stress," I answered.

"Stress! Boy, do I know stress," he said, shaking his head.

Andreí was right! He did know stress. In the distance of three miles, he filled me in on five years of personal history. As I remember, it goes something like this: In 1992 he met and fell in love with a woman. They were married and, within two years, had a baby boy named Anderson. Things started to go bad in the marriage and a year later they divorced.

As it turned out, Andreí got custody of the child. His wife, from Rio de Janeiro, was not a U.S. citizen. Moreover, she had defaulted on several court orders.

For this reason, the judge awarded Andreí custody. His ex-wife had visitation rights. For about two years this situation worked out somewhat well. That is, until one day when Andreí went to pick up his son at his ex-wife's apartment, only to learn that both had left for Brazil two days earlier. Technically speaking, his son had been kidnapped. Andreí hired a lawyer but soon learned that the chances of getting his son back to the States were nil. Inquiries to the State Department were met only with pessimism. The idea of making a trip to Rio proved fruitless. His ex-wife had too many ways to cover her tracks, and in fact had already done so.

Andreí looked heartbroken, yet at the same time defiant.

"How on earth do you deal with this?" I asked.

"I have to accept it. It is out of my hands. I pray to God constantly. I pray for my son's return. I pray he is all right and he will remember me when I see him." Then he paused for a moment. "I have exhausted every possible means. I have no choice now but to accept my fate."

As he finished saying this, the car came to a stop. "Here you are," he said. "Have a good evening."

I paid the fare, stepped out into the pouring rain, and waved good-bye.

As Andreí painfully discovered, there are events in life we have no control over. Try as we might, no amount of money, time, or effort will change a thing in our favor. While determination and persistence are admirable traits, against an immovable object they rob the soul of energy and cause the body unnecessary wear and tear from stress hormones. A Chinese proverb says, "You cannot push water uphill." As difficult as accepting a bad circumstance may be, often it is the only way through it. That day's story served as a stark reminder of how arduous yet essential the lesson of acceptance is so we can move on with our lives.

On the morning of my departure, I wheeled my suitcase into the crowded elevator. When the doors opened at ground level, I approached the reception area, checked out, and patiently waited by the hotel entrance. The bellcap signaled a taxi. I opened the door to see Andreí at the wheel again. He greeted me with a reserved smile.

"You look relaxed," he said, again staring intently at me in the rearview mirror.

"Hi Andreí," I answered. "Good to see you again. How are you?"

"Every day gets a little bit better," he answered, "Every day gets a little bit better." And with that, he stepped on the gas pedal and we were off.

A speaking engagement brought me back to the Windy City recently. Exiting the train station, I flagged a cab. Throwing my suitcase onto the back seat, I climbed in and shut the door.

A distinctly familiar accent greeted me. "Where are you going?" said the driver.

I looked up at the visor to read Andreí's name. Next to his license was that same picture of the Virgin Mary.

"Andreí," I said, "how the heck are you? Any news from your son, Anderson?" It took him a moment to remember my face. Then he broke into a smile.

"Hey, you're the stress guy!" he said. "Yes! Things are a little better. I hear from my son about once a month. He calls collect. There is a chance I may go to Rio in January to see him." Andreí tried to hold back the excitement.

"So tell me, what brings you back to my city?" he asked with a smile.

> Acceptance of a situation does not occur overnight. It is a process we must work through, daily. As this proverb reminds us: "The winds of grace are blowing perpetually, we only need to raise our sails."

2

Ribbons and Tea Bags

I had not spent more than three hours in my position on the faculty of a well-known private university in the nation's capitol when a colleague walked into my office and began to strike up a conversation.

"So, how do you like it here so far?" he inquired.

"Not bad, considering I've only been here a few hours," I replied.

"I don't want to burst your bubble, but it will change," he continued.

I was a bit puzzled, wondering, of course, if I had made a poor decision in accepting this job. "Why?" I asked.

"Well," he said, and then paused for several moments. "Let's just put it this way, the students here whine. They whine a lot!"

I can recall my first reaction. Freud would have described it as denial. Being kinder to myself, I called it "unbridled naiveté."

"Not my students," I said with a smile on my face, believing my own words. "My students won't whine."

My new colleague smiled, patted me on the back, and

said as he walked out, "Welcome."

To my dismay, it didn't take long to find out he was right. My students whined—and they whined a lot. After a month's time, I decided to put an end to it. As part of any good stress-management class, they needed to learn that whining is counterproductive to effectively dealing with stress. So, unabashedly, I banned this behavior. The word went out over campus: *No* whining allowed in Professor Seaward's classes.

To no one's surprise, the class attitude was slow to change, as are most positive health behaviors. So I set out looking for a potent way to remind my students that, by comparison, they actually had a pretty good life. Most students came from wealthy families, some had more expensive cars than the average faculty member, and it is fair to say that the majority of students had, for the most part, lived their lives on the low end of the stress scale. I set out to make this point clear in the classroom.

The nation's capitol is rich in personalities with colorful backgrounds, and I was very fortunate to have met several of these people during my tenure there. One such person was Bruce Laingen. His may not be a household name, but his experience has made an indelible impression on the nation's psyche. As Charge d'Affairs of the American Embassy in Iran, and one of the sixty-five Americans taken as hostages in 1979, Bruce quickly became the group's spokesperson. Eighteen years after his release, I invited him to my class to share how he coped with the stress of his lost freedom for over a year's time in a foreign land.

To set the stage, I went out during lunch and bought several yards of yellow ribbon. My secretary and I cut it up into more than fifty pieces, taping each snippet of ribbon to the wall at eye level all around the room. I decided to make the speaker's appearance a surprise to the class. Students, unaware of his visit, sat curious and silent. As Bruce entered the room, he was quite moved by the sight of fifty-three yellow ribbons, and more than one person saw his eyes well up as he tried to hold back tears.

In an eloquent voice that reminds one of the ageless wisdom shared by sages, Bruce recounted his story. He and his colleagues at the American Embassy in Tehran were rounded up by student terrorists. A handful of workers were released for health reasons over the next few weeks. The final group of captives numbered fifty-three and were held captive for 444 days. As a prisoner, Bruce was often kept in solitary confinement for days. His fate was at the mercy of his captors. Fear, particularly the fear of the unknown, was his prevailing emotion; he never knew when he and his colleagues would be released or even if they would. Initially, the fear of death was very present, too.

He explained that he missed his wife and family terribly. Perhaps this was his greatest stress. Days and nights grew quite lonely. Although separated for days on end from his fellow captives, they developed various tapping codes to communicate with one another. Bruce also tried to understand the perspective of his captors, which he said made their tribulation a bit easier to cope with. The international ordeal ended on the first day President Reagan took office in 1981. Bruce and the fifty-two others were free after nearly fifteen months of captivity.

That day in class, Bruce cited several factors which he felt contributed to his success as a captive prisoner for a year and a half: faith, patience, and optimism were at the top of his list. The students sat mesmerized. Moved by his story, I could already see the changes that would begin to take form in their lives as they gained a new perspective on the meaning of stress.

It is easy to complain about life's shortcomings, and at times we all do. But to get stuck in the habit of whining only attracts more whining. In truth, most of us have it pretty darn good. And, by comparison to people like Bruce Laingen, we have it *very* good. My students got the message. As Bruce reiterated, perspective is essential in dealing with stress.

As he said "Thank you," Bruce pulled a yellow ribbon off the wall, placed it on his lapel, and gave the class a wave of his right hand. The room filled with thunderous applause.

He ended his presentation with a quote that became the motto for our class that semester:

> "Human beings are like tea bags. You don't know your strength until you're in hot water."

3

The Search for Proof

While on a national book tour, I did a book-signing in a large mid-Atlantic city. About thirty people had gathered to hear me share some thoughts regarding the relationship between stress and spirituality. As I began to tell a story, I noticed a man, about thirty-five, dressed in a tie-dyed T–shirt, standing close enough to hear but far enough away to leave without causing any distraction. After standing for twenty minutes, he took a seat. I continued with my discussion, every now and then looking in his direction. His face showed an uncomfortable mixture of anger, disbelief, and a yearning for the truth. Puzzled by his expression, I concluded with the statement that stress is not divine abandonment, but an opportunity for spiritual growth.

When I was done, I asked the audience if they had any questions. The man with the tie-dyed shirt raised his hand, then began to speak.

"What if I don't believe anything you've just said?" he inquired aggressively.

I tried not to look too shocked, but my facial expression

revealed my true feelings. I was stunned. I quickly asked for divine intervention to provide me with a satisfactory answer. It came none too soon.

What I thought to say was that human spirituality isn't a theory but a collection of experiences that more often than not cannot be proven or validated scientifically. Intuitively, I felt he wanted proof. It was then I remembered a story I frequently tell, which I had forgotten to mention. In a visit to Arizona I had a dream in which I met a man who was the son of the woman who hosted my visit. In the dream, he asked me to give his mom a message that he was all right and not to worry. Unbeknownst to me, this son had died of SIDS (Sudden Infant Death Syndrome) more than thirty years before. I had become a messenger of faith.

As I recounted this story, the man's look of anger dissolved completely, only to be replaced by a look of wonder. He appeared to be experiencing a sense of comfort. Then he spoke.

"My wife was killed, brutally murdered, about a year ago. I have spent months trying to make sense of her death, but I have found no comfort in anything I have come across. But just now, the story of your dream reminded of a recent dream I had of my wife. I had completely forgotten it till you mentioned yours. In my dream, my wife came to me, looking young and radiant. She gave me a warm embrace, kissed me, and told me that she was OK, not to worry about her, she was all right. It's funny, but I hadn't remembered that dream until just now. It wasn't a typical dream, it seemed so real." As he said this, a tear welled up in each eye. Not a person in the audience stirred, yet we all knew we had just experienced a rare divine moment.

When it came time to autograph books, the man waited patiently in line until his turn came. He shook my hand with a firm grip and told me his name was Michael. We exchanged glances that spoke more profoundly than words. He thanked me as I signed his book, and then he slowly walked away with the air of confidence that comes from a divine moment, a prayer answered. Michael found his proof and everyone there became richer for it.

> Prolonged anger becomes a dark veil we hide behind for protection. But that which initially protects, over time has the power to hurt us physically and emotionally as well. The search for proof is one way to deal with anger. Keep looking till you find it.

4

A Bird in the Hand

There has been much attention recently regarding the power of prayer. Prayer, it is said, was one of the first coping techniques for stress. When I was young, the prayers I was taught were like poems that were to be recited, primarily in times of need, always in times of trouble. My style of prayer has changed over the years, but the use of prayer as a coping technique in stressful situations hasn't. I pray all the time. As the ancient saying goes, "All thought is prayer," and not a day goes by that I am not consciously praying about something.

Boulder, Colorado, is renowned for its intense summer hailstorms. The carnage is so bad that you may find your car in the auto shop for a week afterwards to get all the dents out. While teaching an evening class one summer night at the University of Colorado, the winds kicked up and sparks of electricity filled Boulder valley. The classroom shook with each clap of thunder, followed by the sound of extremely large hail balls hitting the building. After the initial excitement, I could tell that many of my students were pondering the extent of damage to their cars. So was I. As it was close to the last hour of class, I dismissed the students early and everyone peeled out of the room, taking cover under their textbooks.

Driving home was an ordeal. The voice on the radio alerted listeners to the sightings of three funnel clouds. I, on the other hand, could see almost nothing, even though my windshield wipers were going at warp speed to maintain some degree of visibility.

As I was driving, my thoughts instantly turned to prayer. Not for myself or even for the other drivers who were all moving at a snail's pace on the road. Instead, my thoughts turned toward my bird feeder. Every year a couple of finches build a nest in my bird feeder. This season there were four chicks, about two weeks old. The bird feeder hangs loosely and moves quite freely in the wind. I prayed that those four chicks would survive the terrible storm.

When I got home, the first thing I did was run out to the porch, only to encounter a grim sight. The four chicks were lying dead on the ground. I was saddened as I tried to understand this example of nature's balance.

Early the next morning I peered out my window to see not a hailstone in sight. Within seconds, I observed the parent finches land on the bird feeder, staring at the empty nest. If a bird can have a puzzled look on its face, I surely saw it in theirs. Baffled, both birds flew away. I moved on to other things, pretty much forgetting the whole episode.

Later that night as I walked into my house, I heard a familiar sound—the chirping of baby birds. I rushed outside to see that two chicks were huddled under my porch furniture crying for help. Putting on a glove, I gently picked up each bird and carefully placed it back in the nest, at which point the chirping stopped. That night I prayed that the parents would return once more so they could finish their job.

I woke the next morning to see that one of the two birds I'd rescued had fallen out of the nest during the night and this time really was dead. I sat, waited, and watched the nest for over an hour. Once again I prayed. To my surprise, the parents did return. Now, getting all the attention, the sole surviving bird flourished. Over the next few days it doubled in size.

This family of finches has been renting out my bird feeder for over four years. I have never been known to name the chicks, but this time was different since I had become so intimately involved.

I named the young survivor "Hail Mary"!

> All thought is prayer. In times of stress, may we keep our thoughts filled with positive intentions for the highest good of all concerned.

5

The Healing Power of Prayer

In spring 1997, I was asked to make a presentation on mind-body-spirit healing for the American Occupational Health Association's annual meeting in Orlando, Florida. At first, the crowd of about a hundred physicians seemed less than interested as I stood at the edge of the stage, presenting information on the vanguard of holistic medicine, as part of a one-day stress-management seminar. But the crowd of seemingly uninterested general practitioners became a lively group of participants by the end of the session. As I made my way to the back of the room to pick up my slide carousel, I was politely ambushed by twenty-five physicians and nurses, business cards in hand, asking for more information.

One participant, who patiently waited until the group had dispersed, approached me and said, "You were the reason I came to this conference, but I wished you had talked more about the healing power of prayer. Do me a favor and call Dr. John Pfenninger." She quickly wrote down the man's phone number on the back of her business card, handed it to me, and smiled as she walked away. Intrigued,

I placed a phone call to Midland, Michigan, a few weeks later. Dr. Pfenninger's remarkable story underscores the dynamic healing power of prayer. That afternoon, he shared these memories with me.

In 1994 John's son, Matt, a high school sophomore, was diagnosed with a brain tumor. The diagnosis wasn't immediate. In fact, Matt spent a fair amount of time in and out of hospitals, and if you were to ask him he would tell you that he has seen more than his share of MRI (Magnetic Resonance Imaging) machines. Matt's mother's standing joke is: "The only specialists we didn't consult were those in obstetrics."

Eventually, the diagnosis revealed a brain tumor. It also revealed cancer cells isolated in the fluid of Matt's brain and spinal cord. Matt began to receive the typical treatment: chemotherapy. While often effective, chemotherapy is not infallible. It not only can kill cancer cells but destroys healthy cells as well. And it doesn't always work.

In the shadow of nearly every cancerous tumor lies the question of death. Matt's father decided to meet this shadow head-on. Knowing how much support the Pfenninger family had in this crisis, the thought occurred to John that if Matt were to die, those in attendance at his funeral would be in the hundreds. Rather than have them come together for a funeral, John decided to utilize the energy and well wishes of their friends, colleagues, and family to heal his son, instead of grieving the loss of his life. John called them all to a "gathering to heal."

"I know if Matt were to die right now, you would all come to his funeral, but it makes more sense to me to use your prayers now," John said. "I would like to ask if you could pray with me and my wife for our son to be healed."

So the group of two hundred people sat in silence in an auditorium and prayed for Matt's recovery, some for over an hour. Sixty-five of the 110 physicians on staff attended the prayer meeting.

There are several ways to pray. There are intercessory prayers where we seek help and guidance. There are prayers of gratitude where thanks are given. Many prayers combine supplication for help with offering gratitude. Some prayers read like poems. Some prayers are spontaneous, like ad-lib conversations with God. What all prayers have in common is *intention,* the desire to work in collaboration with a higher source, a display of devotion to join the will of God, in whatever way you imagine that to be.

Several weeks later, Dr. Pfenninger made a grand rounds presentation at his hospital. By all measures, it was a short one. "Many of you have inquired about Matt's condition. As you know, we had a prayer session for him not too long ago. I'd like to show you something." As he said this, he illuminated two X-rays, before and after pictures. The tumor was gone. A hush fell over the crowd.

Jack concluded, "To those of you who understand the power of prayer, no explanation is necessary, and to those of you who do not, no explanation will suffice." With these words and a wave of his hand, Dr. Pfenninger left the stage.

> Not only can faith move mountains, when our will is aligned with the will of God, faith can make tumors disappear. It helps when physicians pray too!

6

Dan's Divorce

It is early Sunday morning, late summer. The rays of sunlight on the Colorado Rockies have turned from pink to orange to white. I sit on my porch enjoying what is known as Alpenglow—sunrise on the Rockies. The phone rings, breaking the silence. I pick up the receiver to hear the shattered voice of one of my best friends, calling from Vermont. My first thought is that his wife or children have been seriously injured. Indeed, this was the case, but the damage was emotional, not physical, with Dan himself bearing the brunt of first impact. As he spoke, he tried to hold back tears, but to no avail. Dan's marriage had capsized and was now shipwrecked on the shoals of infidelity.

Research conducted by Thomas Homes and Richard Rahe in 1967 revealed that divorce is one of the most stressful life events anyone can face, second only to the death of a spouse. I had known Dan to go through a great many harrowing ordeals, but this Sunday morning was truly catastrophic. Sad to say, Homes and Rahe were right!

When we spoke, the story was still incomplete, but the details Dan gave over the phone were enough for me to see the irreversible demise of what both of us thought was a good marriage. As it turns out, Dan's wife had begun a passionate relationship with another man. The affair had become public less than a day before Dan called me. When confronted with the allegations, Dan's wife admitted to her new loyalty and with less than a full explanation, grabbed some personal items, threw them in the car, and drove off to her new lover, leaving her husband and their two young children behind. Shell-shocked, Dan sat down, trying to make sense of a seemingly senseless life-changing event.

Harnessing my best counseling skills, I validated Dan's anger and encouraged him to feel his frustration rather than ignore it, then to try and let it go. With tongue in cheek, he asked permission to quickly move from anger to bargaining, saying she could have the Enya CDs, but the Neil Young collection was staying. We both chuckled. Dan's ability to laugh was, indeed, a good sign.

After an hour or so of sorting through the details, analyzing the personalities of everyone involved, and mourning the loss of a ten-year partnership, Dan had to return to his paternal duties. I promised I would call him back the next day.

In times of strife, a strong support system of friends and family is essential. I did my best, given the distance of two thousand miles, to "be there" for Dan through several phone calls and a barrage of e-mails. When he wasn't connecting with his closest allies, Dan turned inward to do some serious soul-searching.

In the course of several conversations over the next few weeks, I was quite moved by Dan's rapid healing process. I have known friends and colleagues who have gone through similar situations only to get stuck in anger, transforming a dark night of the soul into a decade. It became obvious through our conversations that Dan's faith became the metaphorical biceps muscle to pull him through this crisis.

My Green Mountain friend shared with me what it meant to him to have faith, an undeniable knowing that everything would turn out all right. In turn, I shared with him a favorite quote from Nelson Mandela, from his book *Long Walk to Freedom:* "Faith is not belief without proof, but trust without reservation."

Dan eloquently described to me his conversations with God in which he offered his surrender of personal desires, his intentions of unconditional love for his wife and children, his release of expectations and outcomes, and his promise to walk with God every day.

A quick business trip to Vermont the next spring brought us together over lunch on the banks of Lake Champlain. Our conversation again turned to the subject of faith.

"There are a lot of good stories in the Bible on this subject," I said.

"Yeah, sometimes the 'mustard seed' parable works. On rare occasions when I'm feeling low, I have to resort to something smaller, like a photon of faith," he said with a Cheshire-cat grin. "Just kidding! I typically start with an avocado seed and work up from there."

Even with faith, no stressful event is without its potholes. In Dan's case, there were custody arrangements to be negotiated. The dream house went up for sale. Momentos were boxed up and put in permanent storage, and there were difficult financial adjustments. But through it all, Dan's trust in God—that all would work out—remained constant.

One Sunday morning a full year later, I was again enjoying the sunrise. Again the silence was interrupted by the phone's ring. The Green Mountains and the Colorado Rockies were once more connected. Reviewing the past year, Dan said, "You know, faith is a mystery, but thank God you don't have to understand it to appreciate it!" He added, "The body may need carbs, fats, and proteins, but the spirit requires faith and love. There is no need for anyone to go spiritually hungry. Faith and love are always in abundant supply."

> Faith is not wishing for things to turn out as we would like them to be, although this certainly may happen. Faith is knowing that no matter how things turn out, we will stand strong through the winds of change and walk away gracefully.

7

The Stolen Passport

To know Sandi Lawrence is to know a spiritually minded person. A registered nurse by training and the director of the Student Wellness Office at the University of Southern Indiana (USI), Sandi has dedicated her life to the care and service of others. To know Sandi is also to know an adventurous soul. When she heard that the Mid-American Singers, a choral group from USI, was going to Poland in summer 1997, she made a visit to the office of the choir director and asked, "By any chance, do you need a nurse to go to Poland with you?" Sandi just knew she would be going. He smiled a reassuring Yes. When the choir boarded the plane for Warsaw, Sandi was a welcome addition to the group.

"I felt a little nervous prior to leaving because I didn't know the other people on the trip and I was unfamiliar with the health care delivery system in Poland," she explained. But Sandi did know the potential risks for a bunch of young adults in a foreign country and sought divine help to cover all her bases.

"I have to tell you that I asked many of my friends to

pray for me, that I could take care of the forty people in our group and that I could be the kind of witness to my faith that God would want me to be . . . knowing they were praying for me released me from having to worry about the outcome. I wanted everything to go all right on the trip. And I did my share of praying, too," Sandi explained.

So, how was the trip?

"The trip was fantastic, but it wasn't without its moments," she said.

En route, they had been advised to keep their passports in their possession at all times in a safe place. On the third day, Sandi recalls, one student, Troy, had his passport stolen—pickpocketed, just like you see in the movies.

Sandi quickly surveyed her options. She learned that replacing Troy's passport would require a trip from Gdansk to the American Embassy in Warsaw, causing a disruption of the travel schedule (not to mention undue stress for the thirty-six students and four staff members on the tour). There just wasn't time for unscheduled travel. In her mind, there was no choice: the group had to keep to its original itinerary. Sandi approached Troy and said, "I want you to know that I will be saying prayers that someone brings your passport back to us." A woman of great faith, Sandy started to pray. Pray and detach. She put the whole matter in the hands of God and waited to see what would happen.

On the fifth day in Gdansk, the group decided to take a thirty-minute boat ride to Westerplatte, one of the sites where World War II started. Troy's passport was still missing. The group was to fly home in less than a week.

"So there we were on Westerplatte, overlooking the Baltic Sea, enjoying a sunny day, climbing on tanks and exploring old bombed-out buildings. As I was walking toward the Westerplatte monument, a Polish woman walked up to me and said, 'American?'

"At first, I thought she wanted her picture taken with us, or something like that. I looked at her and said, 'Yes, American!'

"What happened next took my breath away. She proceeded to open her purse and pulled out Troy's passport, then handed it to me.

"'Here,' she said, 'I think maybe this belong to you.'" The woman smiled a faint smile and took a few steps backward.

Sandi quickly called to Troy. When he approached, she told him what had happened and placed the passport securely in his hand. Stunned, Troy said, "This is a coincidence!"

Sandi then asked him if he remembered what she had told him on the bus. Troy answered, "Yes! You said you would be saying prayers until someone brought back my passport."

Sandi exclaimed, "This is not a coincidence, this is an answer to a prayer!"

All the while the group of students proceeded to take pictures of Troy and the Polish woman.

"Now some people would say this is quite a coincidence," said Sandi. "I have no doubt that my prayers, and those of my friends back home, were answered. I came away from this trip with a stronger faith in God and thirty-nine good friends. I think several students did too."

Faith is a unique inner resource to help us in times of need. If stress is a dark tunnel, then faith is the guiding light at the end of it, even if we can't always see it. Faith is a reminder of our divine connection—the assurance that we are neither alone nor abandoned, even in the darkest hour of the darkest tunnel. If there is a recipe for faith, perhaps it is this: one part optimism, two parts confidence, one part wisdom, three parts patience, four parts love, and a pinch of mysticism for good measure. Faith and prayer go hand in hand to serve each other. There are exceptions but, generally, this is how it works.

> Faith, through prayer, can provide some miraculous results, and relieve some stress in the process. An important factor to remember is to detach from the outcome and let whatever may happen do so. Regardless of the result, faith, on the wings of a prayer, can certainly help restore a sense of inner peace.

8

Facing Our Fears Head-On

A *hogan* (pronounced ho-gun) is a type of dwelling common among the Navajo and Hopi tribes. Its architectural structure, a dome-shaped hut with a single entrance and exit that always faces east, is conducive for sweat lodges, a sacred Native American healing ceremony. Today, the healing practice of the sweat lodge has become popular among non-Native American people as well.

Native American culture contains a depth of wisdom that the Western world has yet fully to grasp, particularly in regard to medicinal healing involving diseases such as cancer and AIDS. It was such a case that brought Sam to his first sweat lodge, and his first *hogan* prayer.

How Sam contracted AIDS is not important; his condition was heading downhill as fast as his T-4 cell count. Unconvinced that drugs would help, Sam, like so many others who turn to various forms of alternative medicine and complementary healing, signed up for a sweat lodge ceremony.

If you are unfamiliar with a sweat lodge, there is something you should know. A sweat lodge is not an Indian version of a sauna. In a true sweat lodge, spirits come to offer their healing medicine. This is what Sam was looking for, not just a cleansing but a healing—a purification of his soul.

Others present at the sweat lodge ceremony Sam participated in said that they had never seen the rocks so red before and that the heat was almost unbearable. The medicine woman leading the ceremony recounted later that such intense heat was needed to purify the sickness. After a short while, a spirit spoke. It was the spirit of Thunderbird.

Sam was told to walk outside, strip naked in the rain, and pray. He was to converse and pray to the Thunderbird spirit in a certain way. He was instructed to pray in the *Hayokah* manner, which means praying for the *opposite* of that which you desire. So, if you want to get well, you pray to get worse. If you wish to live, you pray to die.

The *Hayokah* prayer is not easy. For when you pray in this style, you must face your fears head-on. Simply stated, you prepare to fight the metaphorical dragon (a common symbol of fear). This style of prayer forces you to get in touch with that which you most fear and to deal with it directly. The aim is to reduce you to your bare essence—washed clear of any doubts, fears, worries. You begin this prayer alone and end it knowing you are never alone.

After an hour or so, Sam crawled back into the *hogan*. Again he received another message from Thunderbird. He was to stop reading any material about AIDS—no papers, no television, no media that reinforced the message of fear. Again he was instructed to go outside and pray the *Hayokah* prayer. In the pouring rain, Sam faced his fears again till each faded away, never to return.

Six months later Sam happened upon the medicine woman who had conducted his sweat lodge ceremony. His T-4 white blood cell count was back to normal. There was no sign of the AIDS virus. Sam was healed.

Fear is the predominate stress emotion. With the exception of anger, perhaps, all other stress emotions—from doubt and worry to guilt and panic—originate in fear. The most common approach to fear is avoidance, the desire to run and hide. While this may be appropriate for a handful of stressors, it can be devastating with the majority of problems we encounter, no matter how big or small. To confront fear is no easy matter. It takes courage, a word derived from the French, meaning "big heart." Courage is never used to retreat. It is courage that allows us to move through or around our problems, and eventually transcend them.

> In the words of F. D. Roosevelt, "We have nothing to fear but fear itself." We must face our fears to make them disappear.

9

Breakfast with Uncle Fred

It's a well-known fact, if you live in Colorado, that you will find many long-lost friends showing up on your doorstep during ski season looking for free lodging. Some people who come to Colorado during ski season could use a lesson on proper winter attire. No matter what they bring, it never seems to be warm enough. There have been many occasions when I have lent my down ski jacket (luckily, I have two) to a weekend houseguest as the temperature dipped way below freezing. It has almost become a tradition for my guests to reach for my green and purple nylon ski coat before heading out the door.

Several years ago in the cold heart of winter, I reached for "the" jacket myself and hopped into my car to drive to Denver to visit my Uncle Fred. A wealthy man, Fred was the kind of guy who took his role as uncle quite seriously. From my boyhood, I can remember that he was always there with smiles, bear hugs, magic tricks, winks, and an occasional five-dollar bill, which he would stuff in my shirt pocket as he walked out the door. As I headed south to Denver, I secretly thought to myself, in the form of a quick prayer, "Hey, God, I could sure use some of those fives right now." I had just left an academic position to try my hand at consulting. A career change always brings about a change in finances, and my savings were evaporating in the thin mountain air.

Fred's wife Ernie had died of cancer the previous year, and within months of her passing, my uncle was diagnosed with cancer as well. So we met for breakfast and, over omelets and pancakes, discussed some of the deeper issues of life and death, complementary medicine, and the afterlife. Sipping his coffee, Uncle Fred shifted gears and asked me about my career. I decided neither to divulge my financial precariousness nor my massive credit card debt. I assured him I was moderately successful. Quite humbly, I pulled a twenty-dollar bill out of my wallet and picked up the breakfast tab. As the waiter went off to get change, I made a trip to the rest room.

About a month later I got a phone call from my cousin Donna. Fred had died peacefully in his sleep. It was sad news, but I had known his days were short that morning at breakfast. He had so much as told me so.

Two years and many houseguests later, a frigid air mass hovered over the state of Colorado during the Thanksgiving holidays. Bonnie, my fiancée visiting from the east coast, grabbed the green and purple jacket as we headed out the door for a neighborhood walk. Fumbling around the pockets, Bonnie pulled out an envelope, some tissues, some gum wrappers and a Bic pen, looking for the nearest trash barrel. Opening the envelope, she saw a wad of bills and stopped in her tracks. "Look at this," she exclaimed. "There must be several thousand dollars here!"

The first thought that occurred to me was a former

houseguest had misplaced some travel money. After all, this coat had seen several ski resorts in the past two years. We quickly headed back inside and Bonnie counted the money, a total of $3,500. She was stunned. So was I. I started making phone calls to several friends who had borrowed the coat. No one claimed the money. Trying to make sense of it all, I finally found the clue to solving the mystery inside the bank envelope—it was from Uncle Fred!

Over a Thanksgiving feast that same day, I asked my cousin about her father's philanthropic deeds. "Oh," she said, "Dad was always generous, but he was rather quiet about it. On more than one occasion, he would stuff wads of tens and twenties into a bank envelope and place it in my coat pocket when I wasn't around." Then she paused and looked at me, quizzically. "Why? Did he do that with you too?" she asked.

Bonnie and I just smiled at each other. Then we broke out in laughter. That day, Thanksgiving took on a whole new meaning.

> A prayer answered takes time. When we pray, beseeching divine intervention, more often than not we expect immediate results. Human nature may have always been this way, but the age of high technology has certainly brought with it a tacit demand for immediate gratification. No matter what our troubles, there is a higher order to events. And this point is important to remember: All prayers are answered, but in God's time, not ours.

section three

Letting Go of Stress

"LETTING GO OF STRESS" IS A PHRASE USED TO remind us to discard any thoughts, feelings, attitudes, or opinions that no longer serve us. In fact, these perceptions, which at one time might have been quite useful, eventually get in the way of personal goals, cause disruptions in our relationships with our family and colleagues, and limit our own personal growth. Over time, they can become our biggest obstacles in life. In truth, these perceptions are servants of the overinflated ego. They weigh us down and tire us out, eventually impeding our progress on life's journey. Perhaps worst of all, this emotional baggage limits our ability to reach our highest human potential.

What do acceptance, forgiveness, gratitude, and compassion have in common? These are but a handful of ways in which we are invited to open our hearts, temper our egos, and release ourselves from the illusion of control which so often binds us to our problems, perpetuating the stress cycle. Each story in this chapter offers a lesson in letting go and moving on.

"Letting go of stress" is a reminder to do just that—to let go and move on. To stay put is to wither and rot. No one ever said it was easy to let go, but as those who do will tell you, this is where real power and freedom reside.

1

Silver and Gold

There are many definitions of stress, but the definition I have come to appreciate the most is this bit of ageless wisdom: Stress is a disconnection from our divine source. While it's true that we are never separated from God, however we may perceive this connection, unresolved feelings of anger and or fear can become so intense that we actually feel we have been abandoned by the divine. You know what I mean if, in the midst of a crisis, you have ever said to yourself, "What did I do to deserve this?"

While anger and fear are not in and of themselves bad (actually, they are survival emotions), if left unresolved they create what is called in Eastern cultures the veils of illusion. Layer upon layer of these veils eventually obstruct our vision. Ultimately, they create a false sense of separation from our highest self. This is no mere metaphor. It is interesting to note that research reveals that the greater the level of stress we are experiencing, the more our peripheral vision decreases. (And conversely, one great stress-reduction technique is to widen your peripheral vision and peripheral hearing when you feel yourself becoming tense. Stunning, simple, and effective.)

In simplest terms, the ego is the bodyguard for the soul. But in what becomes a never-ending story, the ego exchanges power for control to steal the stage and dominate the show. Motivated by fear, the inflated ego can grow like a cancerous tumor. In truth, the real power resides in letting go. "Surrendering the ego" is an expression used to remind us to detach from earthly desires which impede our spiritual growth.

As a child, my mother would read to me stories, fables, and myths. Not merely entertainment, each tale had a specific message. At the end of the story she would ask me my impressions and what I would do if I was the story's character. Following is one story, as I best remember, which illustrates the idea of surrendering the ego:

Once upon a time, there was a young man who lived in a village surrounded by very tall mountains. On his eighteenth birthday, as was the custom of his people, he packed a sack with clothes and food and, bidding farewell to his family, set out in the direction of the rising sun. As he waved good-bye, he heard his father repeat the words, "Remember the Golden Rule: Do unto others..." but his father's voice faded in the wind. Hurrying off, the young man was eager to get going on his mission, which was to discover the nature of his being, seek his life fortune, and, if his fate so dictated, to one day return to his village bearing gifts of treasure and great wisdom from faraway lands.

One day well into his voyage, he heard the cries of an old elf-like man, apparently stuck at the bottom of a deep well. Only his feathered cap lay at the well's stone edge. The tiny man had fallen in an attempt to get a drink. With no rope, he could not climb out. "Fetch me out of this well and I will pay you with a piece of silver," he said to our hero. The traveler, assuming this might be a trap, offered no help. Seeing a small heavy sack on the ground beside the well, he picked it up, placed it in his satchel, and continued on his way, passing though several villages and hamlets. The sack, he was to learn that evening, was filled with nuggets of gold. This will be useful, he thought, as he lay down to sleep among the stars, clutching his newfound treasure tightly in his arms.

In the tenth month of his journey, the young man sat down to rest by a stream. Cooling his bare feet in the water, he was startled by a beautiful maiden picking wildflowers. In their exchange, she offered him a silver ring as a token of good luck for his trip. The young man was unimpressed. He had acquired a taste for gold. In fact, in a bet with a French troubadour he'd encountered a week earlier, he had won twelve more golden nuggets. Silver is of no real value, he told himself. My mission is to acquire more gold. The Golden Rule, as he'd come to understand it, was: "He who has the gold, rules!"

Bidding the maiden farewell, he placed his shoes back on his feet and headed toward the next town. On his way, he met a gnarled old beggar woman by the side of the road. Her face was bleeding and she'd obviously been beaten and left for dead. Only her silver-handled walking stick remained by her side. Hand outstretched, the old hag pleaded for assistance. The young man began to reach for a piece of gold, but sensing this might be a trap, instead pulled a polished stone from his coat pocket, placed it in the her hand, and, without wishing her well, continued walking toward the village. Within a fortnight he had accumulated twenty more golden nuggets.

On the next leg of his journey, the young man came to a river. The water was moving too quickly for him to ford it, so he waited for a ferry to take him safely across. Within a short time, the ferry arrived and he boarded, paying the old ferry master a modest amount for safe passage. No sooner did the flat ferryboat reverse direction than it hit a large rock under a torrent of waves, and the ferry master was thrown overboard. The young man was about to offer assistance when the large raft tilted. Burdened with the weight of the gold-filled sack on his belt, the young man plunged overboard into the raging whitewater along with the ferry master. Now, even though he was a fair swimmer, he tired quickly as his large bag of gold weighed him down. Seeing this, the old man yelled, "Take off your belt and grab my hand!" The young man rued the loss of his treasure, but he feared his death more. So he unbuckled his belt, losing the gold fortune he had amassed, and soon was strong enough to fight the current and climb aboard the boat. As he dried himself off in the sun, he turned to see the aged ferry master climb aboard. Before his eyes, the old man transformed into the beautiful maiden of the forest. In her one hand was the silver ring, the other held the old beggar woman's walking stick. The young man fell to his knees, humbled, for he understood his mistaken behavior and was filled with remorse.

As the boat neared the shore, the fair maiden once again handed the young man the silver ring. He stepped ashore, gave her thanks for his safe passage, and headed west into the mountains toward his village. Now he was ready to go home and share his true fortune—the Golden Rule: Do unto others as you would have them do unto you. He vowed to commit his life to acts of service, and by sunset that very day he had done three. Arriving in the village the next day, he was greeted by his parents and friends. Behind the crowd stood the fair maiden, whom he married by year's end.

> EGO stands for "Edging God Out." When you surrender your ego, you bring the divine spirit back into your heart, and no matter what is happening in your life, it is easier to bear.

2

The Case of the Delayed Flight

The entire range of human emotions can be seen on any day at any airport, from exuberant smiles and tears at the reunion of loved ones to the hypertensive scowls on the faces of passengers receiving news of a delayed flight. Being a frequent flyer, I see the entire range every time I travel, but one day stands out, wing and tail, from the rest.

On a trip from San Jose, California, to Denver, I stood patiently in line for the next ticket agent to stamp my ticket. No stranger to the "friendly skies," this employee was determined to share her smile with every customer. Sensing she was a good sport, I engaged in a conversation about professional travel. When she inquired if I had any bags to check, I placed my tongue in my cheek and said, "No, but I do have some emotional baggage."

Without skipping a beat, she said, "Remember, only two carry-ons."

We laughed. I passed through security and found my way aboard flight #1602. As luck would have it, I had been upgraded to first class. Comfortably seated, I reclined with a glass of orange juice and patiently waited for the plane to push away from the gate.

Once all the passengers were seated, the flight attendants began to demonstrate emergency procedures. Then they took their seats and we waited. Twenty minutes later, the pilot's voice came over the speaker.

"Eh, folks, I don't know how to tell you this, but there is a federal agent on board who has lost an item. Consequently, everyone needs to exit the plane and go through security again—including your carry-on bags."

Moans of incredulity swept the cabin. One man in front of me said in all seriousness, "This is a conspiracy. I watch The X-Files, I know what's going on."

No one laughed but me. Perhaps everyone else had connections to think about. Sheeplike, we filed off the plane and proceeded to go once again through the security check-in.

Once back in the terminal, it was easy to see how stressed the secret service agent, a young man about twenty-five, was feeling. Apparently he was missing his gun, which he had in his possession when he boarded. Now it was gone. After twenty minutes of standing in line, we were given the go-ahead to board the plane again, and within an hour of our initial departure we were up in the air. Rumors quickly spread through the line of disgruntled passengers like a game of grade-school "telephone"—"He found the gun!" "I think it was an Uzi!"

After the in-flight meal, I walked up toward the galley and struck up a conversation with a flight attendant. After making a brief comment about the meal, I inquired about the missing gun.

"Well, we're not supposed to say, but it looks like it was

stolen." Yikes, I thought. As if she read my mind, she added, "It could have been scary, but everything is OK."

The threat of a hijacking was over, but the threat of missed airline connections was very real to nearly everyone on board the plane. Tension hung heavy in the air.

If there is one thing I have learned about traveling, it is that when you become a passenger, you relinquish control of your arrival. All you can do is sit back and relax.

> God, grant me the serenity to accept the things I cannot change, the courage to change the things I can, and the wisdom to know the difference (particularly on airplane rides).

3

Passing Judgment—Not a Good Thing to Do!

A while ago, I was asked by my textbook publisher to write a series of human interest feature stories for a college textbook on drug abuse. I had used the format for my text on stress management and the appeal was so great that my editor decided to use a similar approach for this new book project.

I approached the idea with hesitation. Never having used drugs of any kind, I felt I was the wrong person for this project. Stress, I knew. Drugs were a foreign concept. My editor was unyielding.

"You teach college, right? Interview some of your students. I'm sure they have a lot of firsthand experience," he said with a chuckle as he concluded the conversation. Pondering the possibilities, I agreed, but not without reservations. The revised edition of this drug textbook was scheduled to have seventeen chapters, covering the full range of drug use, from cigarettes to cocaine. My assignment was to find one person per chapter and write up a human feature story for each.

The next night of my class —I was teaching a course on nutrition—I explained to my students my new assignment, and a handful of students accepted the invitation. Several telephone interviews later, I had come up with about sixteen drug-related stores, one shy of my self-imposed goal. So I returned to my class looking for one more story. Right before I was to start into my lecture, a student came whizzing into the classroom on his skateboard, then flipped the board into his hand as he took a seat in the back row. I knew with one glance that I had found my last story. Perched on his chair, wearing a tie-dyed shirt and peering through wire-rim glasses, Chris looked dazed and confused—and I hadn't yet started the lecture. When it came time for a break, I walked over to him and asked if he would see me after class. Bewildered, he agreed.

As the students filed out of class, Chris walked up to me, skateboard in tow. He ran a hand through his long, frizzy black hair and stood patiently as I packed up my notes.

"Chris," I said, "this has nothing to do with class." I paused, searching for the right words. "I need a favor." Chris listened attentively as I explained that I needed one more feature story for the drug text. When I finished explaining, he agreed without hesitation to be interviewed. I took down his phone number, set up a time to call him, and then we both walked out the door. It was rather hard to tell what Chris was feeling, but I was elated. In my mind, this kid had the word "drugs" written all over his face.

Four days later, I dialed his phone number.

"Hello, is this Chris?" I asked.

"Just a sec, I'll get him," the voice answered.

"Hello, Chris?" I said again.

"Yeah, this is Chris. How ya doing?"

"Good! Are you ready for the interview?"

"Sure, let's start."

"OK," I began, "tell me any experiences you've had with drugs—pot, coke, alcohol." I usually started with this question to see if there was a tendency toward one particular drug.

"Well, I really don't do those kinds of drugs."

I shook the phone for a better connection.

"Did you ever smoke pot?" I inquired.

"Once, but I didn't really like it," came his reply.

"What about booze, are you a beer drinker?" I persisted.

"When I was a kid, I tried a beer, but I never liked the taste. Actually, I don't drink at all."

Flustered with how the interview was going, I changed tack quickly in the hopes of finding one more story. "Chris, how about your friends? Do they do recreational drugs?"

"Not really, I don't hang around those kinds of guys, I guess."

"Well," I concluded optimistically, "Chris, I'll try to do something with this, but I can't promise anything."

Chris replied, "OK, but don't you want to know about Ritalin? I thought that's what you wanted to talk about."

I was stymied and somewhat embarrassed. Ritalin? I was so focused on recreational drugs that I stupidly passed over prescription drugs. Worse, I had made a judgment about this student which was totally false. He may have looked like a Grateful Dead groupie, and he might have been, for all I know, but a hard-core drug user? Definitely not!

The ego loves to judge and evaluate. It's extremely good at this. Perhaps good to a fault. In a sense, judgment is like an internal alarm sensor. While at times this thought process may be necessary, perhaps even life-saving, most of the time judgment just gets in the way of happiness and diminishes our ability to connect with others. But a strong ego is always on guard, ready to judge, particularly when it comes to other people's looks and behaviors that are different from our own.

Freud called this behavior "projection," a defense mechanism of the ego to protect or minimize our own emotional pain in a given situation. In simple terms, judgment we place on others is often a projection of our own fears, prejudices, and insecurities. Because it would be painful to admit these to ourselves, we project our perceptions onto other people, often unaware that we are doing it. So, in truth, those we judge are really reflections of ourselves, or perhaps stated more accurately, they represent specific qualities of ourselves that, in a candid moment, we would have to admit are none too flattering. Passing judgment on others is a common stress-prone behavior. It's an area in which we could all use a little reminder to drop the gavel and relax.

I was chagrined at my judgment of Chris, but if there were any ill feelings on his part, he never showed it. I learned a valuable lesson that day. I remind myself regularly of its importance. Although it may seem all too easy to pass judgment on scores of people with whom we come in contact, it's definitely not a good idea.

Every face you meet is the face of God. Every face you meet is a reflection of yourself. Accept the beauty and diversity of all people and the beauty of your inner self will shine.

4

Walking in Balance

In a recent survey, time and money (or, more accurately, the lack thereof) were cited as the two most common stressors for Americans. As both work and home responsibilities increase, the pressure to do more and do it well can lead to a perpetual feeling of tension and frustration. The end result is a hectic lifestyle best described as "out of balance."

The behaviors of hunting and gathering are as present today as they were for our ancestors; now, however, there is a slight twist. Living in a competitive consumer society, the race is on to accumulate "things," which in turn, only adds to the time and money pressures. Ideas for time management are as plentiful as grains of sand in an hourglass, but one thing experts agree on is that rather than finding one more hour in the day, we must learn to use the hours we do have more efficiently. This often means deleting things so we may live a more balanced life.

Mary is a single working mother of three children, all under the age of ten, and not a day goes by that she doesn't experience some level of stress. She loves her job, and although she admits to being rather biased, says her children are quite well behaved. The stress comes from too many responsibilities and not enough time to get everything done in the course of a very long day. "Between walking the dog, dance lessons, swim team, and day care, not to mention my job, by the end of the day I am like the Energizer Bunny whose batteries have died," she laughs.

Mary is a spiritual woman, and her moments of inspiration come from the Bible. Years ago she got into the habit of using the Bible as an oracle. Opening to a random page, Mary closes her eyes and lets her index finger land on a word, typically loaded with a divine message. "Sometimes," she laughs, "I point to the word *the* or *and* and I have to do it over again."

"But let me tell you something," she explains as her eyes grow wide. "Since my divorce three years ago, things have not been easy, but last month was by far the worst. I was beyond patience and my gas tank of faith was running on fumes. So, in my typical fashion, I walked over to the Bible, prayed for a message, and this time, I got a doozy. There under my finger was the word *balance*. I knew immediately what the message referred to, and boy, did I need to hear it."

Mary proceeded to explain that her life had become top-heavy with responsibilities. "My life was like a boat ready to tip over. Something had to get thrown overboard so that my ship would come back upright again. So I sat down with the children that night and explained my strategy. We all came to an agreement. We would simplify our lives, not complicate the family structure with our rendition of Camp Runamok. We set limits on watching television. Each kid agreed to take only one sport or hobby, not the usual three. We decided to cook more meals at home and eat out less. I placed better boundaries around my work schedule. It's been three weeks now and my life—our lives—have come to a place of balance. I think I fell into the trap where I was trying to please everyone and, in the process, pleasing no one. There comes a point every now and then when you have to edit your life to regain a sense of balance, and my time was long overdue."

"This morning I picked up the Bible and opened it again. You know what word my finger found?" Mary said with a smile.

"Peace."

Balance is crucial to nature and fundamental to a healthy life. There are reminders of balance everywhere, and it is not hard to achieve. Make it a goal to strive for balance each day.

5

Life and Death in a Small Town

How do you explain death to a little child? Using words they think their children will understand, parents often describe death as a journey or a trip from which a person just doesn't come back. The death of a house pet often provides teachable moments for children as they try to process the difference between life and death, animate and inanimate, and the here and hereafter. The meaning of death through old age or an accident is already somewhat difficult to explain; death from murder or suicide pushes the limits of grace in a teachable moment. Of all the events played out on the human stage, the death of someone close to you is cited as the most stressful episode anyone can experience.

In the fourth grade I had a good friend name Timothy Silly. Tim was a shy, quiet kid. He never spoke out in class. He never did much to bring attention to himself. He did confide in me that he hated his last name. That was attention enough. He was teased unmercifully. Still water runs deep, though: what Tim may have lacked in extrovert qualities, he made up for with intelligence. He was the kind of kid who always knew the right answers. During recess we would hang out and talk, kick a soccer ball, or just walk around the schoolyard. Looking back, it seems to me that Tim was a troubled soul. Decades have passed and I am often reminded that you can see someone every day, at work, at school, and never really know what goes on in their life. Such was the case with Tim.

One day I came to school and noticed that Tim wasn't sitting at his desk. He didn't come the next day, either. On the third day, the teacher made an announcement. She said that Tim wouldn't be in class anymore. She never mentioned his name again. I was a little confused, but thought perhaps he had moved away. It would be like Tim not to say much about this. Getting him to talk about much of anything was like pulling teeth.

I remember shuffling home that day, sad that I had lost a friend. I walked into the house to overhear my mother on the phone. Her voice conveyed a sense of shock. I heard her mention Tim's last name and the words murder and suicide. At that point she saw me enter the kitchen, said she had to go, and hung up the phone. I stood there with a blank look on my face.

That afternoon I received my first lesson about death. I don't remember the exact words my mother used, but as delicately as she could, she explained to me that Tim's father had tatim his own life, but not before killing his wife and two children. I would never see or hear from Timothy again.

I have thought of Tim many times over the years, particularly when similar events make the headlines. Such an act of violence makes as little sense to me now as it did then. Not long ago, in preparing a presentation on the healing power of humor, I learned this: the word *silly* comes from the Latin word *selig*. It means "blessed" or "holy." I took a moment to reflect on my friendship with Tim. I wish I could have told him then what I learned about being silly. I think he would have liked its meaning. From this experience I have also learned much about tolerance, for one never truly knows another person's experiences which can greatly affect their mood and personality.

> Perhaps the greatest lesson is that there are many circumstances and catastrophes which make absolutely no sense. Try as we might, we can find little or no meaning in them. Some may say it is "God's will," but this leaves us with little consolation. There is still a void where there was once life, pain where there was joy. Devastating events such as plane crashes and earthquakes, or a murdered child, deepen the sense of loss. In time, the wounds will heal, but they lend very little to our understanding of "why." It is fair to say that we will never have the answers to all of life's questions. Yet the void is never filled by staying still. We must move on.

6

A Moving Meditation

There is a life-force of subtle energy which surrounds and permeates everything. The Chinese call this life force *chi*. To harmonize with the universe, to move in unison with this energy, to move as freely as running water, is to be at peace, one with the universe. The ancient practice of t'ai chi is a graceful exercise bringing one in harmony with nature and the universe.

I first started practicing t'ai chi, which is sometimes called "moving meditation," in graduate school, intrigued by its apparently mystical nature. Later, when I began teaching stress-management classes, I knew that this was one technique I wished to share with my students. Perhaps more profound than the exercise itself is the Taoist philosophy underlying it. In simple terms, Taoism speaks of balance. It is often symbolized by the well-known symbol of a half-black, half-white circle; in each half there is a small dot of the opposite color.

Taoism honors the union of polar opposites (for instance, male/female, hot/cold, day/night), referred to as yin and yang. When these opposites come together, they don't fight in opposition. Rather, they unite to create wholeness; you can't have one without the other. The Tao is the unseen, mystical force which energetically binds all things together. Taoism gently reminds us of greatness through humbleness, strength through softness, power through gentleness, wisdom through nature, prudence through discretion, and insight through patience. Indeed, the principles of Taoism are identical to the concepts of stress management.

In the practice of t'ai chi, one learns to move in rhythm with energy, to go with the flow. The same philosophy can be applied to life's daily routines as well. Rather than continually fighting resistance, trying to change things we have absolutely no control over, the implicit message is to flow like water. Internal strength grows from passivity, receptivity. As a physical metaphor, t'ai chi reminds us to stand strong while going with the flow. But t'ai chi offers other benefits as well.

Betty Stewart heard of t'ai chi more than twenty years ago, but it wasn't until September 1994, when she was seventy-nine years old, that she began to practice it in earnest. In the early '70s she was intrigued to try this form of relaxation, and even went out and bought a video so she could teach herself, but she said that it just didn't work. Then one day, years later, Betty noticed that a t'ai chi class was to be offered at the Prestige Club, a unique hospital-based health promotion program for seniors in Colorado, which has a special focus on bridging standard and complementary forms of healing. Betty wasted no time in signing up.

What makes Betty's story so remarkable are the changes she noticed after she began taking the class. Prior to beginning the course, Betty was all of fifty-five inches tall. To the amazement of her physician, she has gained over two inches in height since she began to practice t'ai chi. And, unlike most people her age who lose inches to bone demineralization, Betty's bone density has actually increased in the two years she has been doing t'ai chi. Recently she told me, "There was a chance to be involved in a bone demineralization study, but I said I didn't have time in my life to see if after four years of clinical trials, all I got was the placebo. I wanted the real thing; that's why I started t'ai chi."

Aside from the increase of bone integrity, Betty says there have been other benefits. "I have a much better sense of balance. Why, one day I tripped on an uneven sidewalk. Because I had learned how to shift my weight, all that happened was a little bang, no fracture. My coordination and concentration skills have also improved, as has my level of energy. You know, you cannot do t'ai chi if your mind wanders. You lose track of where you are in the progression of movements."

Besides the physical movements, Betty is attracted to the philosophy of this moving meditation. "There is a real poetic quality to t'ai chi," she says with a smile in her voice. "I can tell you about stress too! Let's just say that both me and my husband have had our fair share of it these past few years. T'ai chi has really kept me balanced. I think t'ai chi is phenomenal."

Recently Betty has become more than a practitioner of t'ai chi—she is a roving ambassador for it as well. As part of the Prestige Plus Program of her hospital in Longmont, Colorado, she now travels to assisted living centers and teaches her peers how to do t'ai chi. There are over thirty-seven movements to master in the traditional short program, but Betty felt this was too much for seniors to learn, particularly those in wheelchairs. So, with the help of her teacher, she created a special short routine, known affectionately as the "Cinnamon Park Form."

"There are people in wheelchairs who wish to do some part of t'ai chi, but they are limited in their motion because they are seated. So I made up a short form of t'ai chi they could do."

Over the phone one afternoon, Betty told me that t'ai chi isn't just another form of exercise, it's become a way of life for her.

> Mountains and water may not have much in common, but when combined, they offer the message of majestic strength and calm gentleness. To be strong, solid, and secure during the winds of change, yet able to move peacefully like running water over rocks and shoals—this is the message of t'ai chi, this is the message of the Tao, and this is the message of managing stress.

7

Sweet Forgiveness

Much stress is caused by deep-rooted anger and resentment, poisons that, left unattended to, corrode our system, literally making us sick. That's why part of an effective stress-management program involves practicing forgiveness. Forgiveness is a component of the human spirit that acts as a bridge to connect the mind and body. If unresolved anger is toxic to the spirit, then forgiveness is the antidote. Where anger is an insurmountable roadblock, forgiveness serves as a tall ladder to climb above and transcend the experience. For forgiveness to be complete and unconditional, we must be willing to let go of all feelings of anger, resentment, and animosity. Sweet forgiveness cannot hold any taste of bitterness—the two are mutually exclusive.

Joanne is a physician living in the southeast corner of the country. Although trained in Western medicine, Joanne's intuitive side brought her to the front door of the field of Psychoneuroimmunology (PNI), where mind, body, and spirit meet in the dynamics of human life. Like most people who become physicians, she entered the field because of her desire to help people. Pain is one of the things that physicians try to alleviate in their patients, and Joanne is no stranger to pain.

In 1997, the back and neck pain she had been experiencing for over a decade became so intense that she literally could not sit. She tried a host of known modalities in her profession to cure it—pills, physical therapy, acupuncture, craniosacral therapy—none of which seemed to work. One day she awoke to find that her right hand and arm were numb. An MRI revealed several bone spurs in her neck, distorting the spinal cord. A neurosurgeon detected nerve damage clear down to her feet. On his advice, she reluctantly scheduled herself for surgery.

"I did not want to go through with the operation," she explained to me at a workshop. "I am well aware of the mind-body connection, and as I lay there I wondered why the mind-body techniques I practiced—mental imagery, etc.—didn't kick in.

"One day I was lying on my living room floor listening to the Caroline Myss tape *Why People Don't Heal,* in which she was talking about forgiveness as a key element to the healing process. I asked myself, 'Who do I have to forgive?' I combed my past to see what lay lurking in the shadows, some unfinished business that I had yet to attend to. Then it came back to me."

In 1984, Joanne and her boyfriend Lee took a trip to Grand Cayman Island. Toward the end of their stay, they rented a car and drove to a remote beach, a romantic, secluded paradise.

Late that afternoon, while combing the beach for shells, they were accosted by a man with a knife who had murder on his mind. In a bloody fight for their lives, both

Joanne and Lee were badly beaten and stabbed. A swift kick to the face of their assailant finally allowed them to escape and get help, but the emotional trauma later manifested as Post-Traumatic Stress Disorder for both Joanne and Lee.

"I came to see that I was hanging on to some remnant of this event and it had become immobilizing. So I lay there sending thoughts of forgiveness to this man. I prayed for forgiveness and then I sent thoughts of forgiveness to myself. As I did this, I noticed the pain became less severe. I knew immediately this was the connection. So I continued with this. Although I had previously wished my assailant dreadful tortures in prison, what was called for was unconditional forgiveness. I felt that knives would no longer be a part of my life. I believed that the bone spurs had been zapped. As I lay there, I was overtatim by a joy more profound than any I have ever known."

Joanne explained to me that there isn't a doubt in her mind that her condition was related to the feelings of resentment she harbored for her assailant. Now it was time to let go. Having done so, the end result was, as it always is, wholeness. Her neck pain never returned.

"I would like to thank my forgiveness, which *A Course in Miracles* defines as the realization that we are not separate—that everything is connected. What was once a curse is now a blessing, for which I am forever grateful. I hope to share this lesson with many others."

> Forgiveness is one path of the healing process. Unresolved anger is a toxin to the spirit, forgiveness is the antidote. Every act of forgiveness is an act of unconditional love, and it is through this love that inner peace resides.

8

Making Friends with the Enemy

In the early 1980s I took a job at a hospital working in the Cardiology Department. As any nurse will tell you, there is an abundance of overinflated egos within the walls of any hospital. In fact, the tongue-in-cheek definition of M.D. is "Medical Deity." This hospital was no different. Before I even took the position, I had heard mixed reviews of the particular person I was to work under. However, I was committed to giving him the benefit of the doubt. My doubt soon waned. It didn't take more than a few days to see the truth, even through my rose-colored glasses. Back in the early '80s the expression "boss from hell" hadn't been coined. Instead, everyone just referred to this guy as the "Antichrist."

Intimidation was his *modus operandi*. His gaze was piercing. No matter how well you did your job, it was never good enough. He was quick to criticize and even quicker to undermine efforts which did not support his means. There was no room for creativity and no tolerance for different opinions. And it is no exaggeration to say that there was no life outside of work. We were all at his beck and call every hour of the day.

I was quick to learn that every conversation on and off premises was consumed by this one personality. Topics about the weather, sports, politics, and religion all funneled down to the subject of the boss from hell. To make matters worse, I was asked on a daily basis how I could stand him. Some people simply asked, "How do you like your job?" waiting for me to complain about him.

But for me, pessimism serves little purpose. Constantly complaining never solves anything. In fact, it tends to intensify feelings of anger and animosity, which, in turn, perpetuate the stress response rather than resolve it. Rather than place my neck in the noose of negativity, I devised a strategy. I decided to give a standard response. I would answer by saying, "This job has proven to be a valuable learning experience." More than once I saw eyeballs roll back in disbelief, but I held firm to my perception. As it turned out, I did learn a lot from this guy. I learned how not to administrate a program. I learned how not to treat employees. In essence, I learned how *not* to be a boss from hell.

I often look back on my career and silently give thanks to my boss from hell. He proved to be a great teacher, perhaps far greater than he'll ever know. From this and many other experiences, I have come to realize that if we can learn from even the most difficult situations, there is some value to them. And with value, even the most negative situation turns out to have a positive side. Perhaps the world-renowned mythologist Joseph Campbell said it best: "Jesus said love your enemies, he didn't say don't have any."

Gratitude is the door to forgiveness. By giving thanks to those from whom we have learned, we cross the threshold of forgiveness.

9

Two Monks and a Woman

There is an expression which says, "Where there is ego, there is stress." That's why sages throughout the ages have offered the same advice to deal with ego-produced stress: detach, release, and surrender the ego. Most of us, however, hang on and cling to stress-producing thoughts which, in fact, no longer serve our purpose. Prejudice, guilt, grief, and doubt, to name a few, have a heavy gravitational pull on the human soul. Hanging on to old thoughts, attitudes, perceptions, and beliefs stunts our mental, emotional, and spiritual growth. While at first they may be useful to get through a given situation, old perceptions gather weight as we attempt to move forward in our lives. Some perceptions act like roadblocks, disrupting the journey altogether. To break the cycle, we must constantly remind ourselves to let go of a perception that has outlived its time and in this way let go of the stress.

To remind myself of this, I always like to keep the following story from the Zen tradition in mind. Two monks were walking from one town to the next on a humid summer day. In silence, they walked for miles under the hot sun along a graveled path. Late in the afternoon, they sat down on the grass and listened to the sounds of water cascading over stones in a shallow riverbed. If the monks kept their pace, they would reach their destination before sunset. After a short while they got up and resumed the trek. Soon they came upon the remains of a washed-out bridge. Built several years previously, it had been destroyed in spring floods. Without thought, the first monk stepped into the water and proceeded to make his way across the river, careful of his footing; the second monk followed ever so cautiously.

Upon reaching the far bank, the first monk looked up to see a woman approach him. "The bridge is washed out and I cannot make it across and I must get to my village before dark. What am I to do?" she cried.

The first monk offered to carry her back across the shallow water. Picking her up, he carefully secured each step until he placed her down safely on dry land. Then he turned around and forded the stream once more to join his fellow traveler.

The two again walked for miles in silence, until the first monk paused for a moment and then sat down. The second monk sat by his side and began to speak.

"Brother, we have tatim vows of chastity. How could you pick up that woman and carry her as you did? You have forsatim your vows," he admonished.

The first monk answered, "Remember, we have also tatim vows of service." He paused for a moment and then said,"Brother, I left that woman on the banks of the river several miles ago. It is you who still carry her."

Carrying around useless stress is a heavy burden to both body and soul. Remember to travel light on your journey of life.

10

Never Again!

One day, while I was standing alongside the swimming pool, ready to start my workout, a man twice my age walked up to me and, in an accent I couldn't place, asked if he could share my lane. His smile was genuine and I could have sworn I saw one of those Hollywood twinkles in his eyes. Getting in the water is by far the worst part of swimming, so in an effort to stall the chilling effects of immersion just a moment longer, I nodded my head and waved him in ahead of me. In he plunged, and for the next fifty minutes he never paused once to rest along the pool's edge. I was intrigued by his good nature, not to mention his stamina, and hoped to strike up a conversation at the end of our workout. As I approached the wall to do a flip turn, he tapped me on the foot, waved good-bye, and jumped out of the water, heading for the locker room. By the time I finished my workout, he was gone.

Several days passed before I saw him again. Once more he approached me, motioned to my lane, and this time, without saying a word, dove in and started swimming. As he entered the water, I noticed a tattoo on his left forearm.

Throughout my workout, I was puzzled by the engraved numbers, distantly familiar, yet beyond my immediate recognition. In fact, it bothered me all day long. Just as fast as he entered the water, he jumped out fifty minutes later, but not without tapping my foot, waving good-bye, and smiling.

My curiosity now heightened, I began to ask around about this man's identity. I learned that, like me, he was a faculty member of American University. His name was Arnost Lustig. He had a very different past, however.

Originally from Poland, Arnost was about seventeen when he and his family were rounded up by the German Nazis and sent off to the notorious concentration camp, Auschwitz. Like all prisoners who entered that camp, he was separated from his family, stripped of all his belongings, robbed of his essence, and denied his humanity. I was told by those who knew Arnost that the horrors of Auschwitz can never be put satisfactorily into words. The tattoo I observed on his forearm was his official identification number. About a year after he was interned there, the American Forces liberated the camp and hell came to a gradual end. Arnost was a free man in a world riddled with chaos and grieving lost innocence. Like many Holocaust survivors, he emigrated to the United States to start a new life.

The next time I saw Arnost it was in the pool locker room. He approached me and introduced himself to me. We exchanged names and then he gave me a big hug, kissed my forehead, and, with another big smile and twinkle in both eyes, said, "You are like a son to me!" On that day we started a budding friendship, enjoying several workouts and conversations. I later learned that his last name, Lustig, means "humor" or "laughter" in German. It is a name he wears well. Putting his hand to his mouth, he whispered, "It's how I got through that horrible ordeal in Auschwitz." Then he put his arm around me and proceeded to tell me a joke.

Until the day I met Arnost, the Jewish Holocaust was a distant event in history to me. From the film footage I saw in high school to the works of psychologist Victor Frankl to Steven Speilberg's *Schindler's List,* the stories of the Holocaust were disturbingly moving. Yet it wasn't until that day that Hitler's "Final Solution" became a living memory. For those who survived, it is said that the atrocities of the Jewish concentration camps were the worst hell on earth.

The same semester I met Arnost, one of my undergraduate students shared with me a story during a classroom discussion about anger and forgiveness. Her grandmother, also a concentration camp survivor, had moved to New Jersey after the war. She returned to Europe two decades later with her daughter. Crossing a street in Poland, she saw the face of a man she could never forget, a Nazi concentration camp supervisor. Filled with emotion, the woman grabbed her daughter's hand and walked over to the man, with the intention of slugging him. As she got within a foot of the decrepit old man, she looked him straight in the eyes and quickly changed her mind. Instead she said "I forgive you," then slowly turned and calmly walked away.

Recently my intrigue with Holocaust survivors led me to Nick Del Calzo's book *The Triumphant Spirit,* a collection of portraits and stories of Holocaust survivors. Although the common theme of hope, the internal sense of a positive outcome, is evident among all survivors, there emerges another theme as well—forgiveness. Many survivors explained it this way: we had to learn to forgive and move on. To hold disdain and hatred toward a person or a people for such horrible atrocities only perpetuates hatred.

There are many lessons to be learned, and forgiveness is one of them. In the words of Auschwitz survivors Paula and Klauss Stern, "We didn't survive to hate—but to hope that the world learned something from the experience, so that atrocities like these will never happen again."

> Yom Kippur, the Day of Atonement, is an important Jewish holiday. It is a day to make peace with our mistakes, injustices, and wrongdoings. Although it is not a national holiday, many of my students excuse themselves from class to honor the day. I honor the day, too. For me it is a day of forgiveness, and a day to remember.

11

Compassion in Action

At the first sign of stress, my sister Gail would light up. The cigarette dangling from her mouth started as an occasional social habit in college. With the advent of her first job as a graphic artist, however, it soon became an adult version of a baby's pacifier. Like most people who smoke, Gail tried passionately to quit but her efforts met with little success. More than once I would hear her quote Mark Twain, "Quitting smoking is easy, I've done it hundreds of times." Eventually, social pressures at work forced her to take her adaptive coping technique outdoors, yet the habit continued.

As Gail explained to me, "Cigarette smoking is horribly addictive. The craving for a smoke, actually it's the nicotine, is beyond approach. I have had other addictions, which we won't go into, but this has got to be one of the hardest."

When Gail was pregnant with her first child, Ashley, she kept the consumption of cigarettes to a strict minimum. "I would catch flak from some people—nonsmokers who haven't a clue. My friends who smoke were more compassionate." With her second pregnancy she did even better; yet old habits die hard. Within a month of giving birth to her son Ian, Gail was back to a pack-a-day habit.

"I am very careful not to light up around my children. I know the dangers of secondhand smoke. I don't smoke in the house or the car. And you wouldn't believe the nagging I get from my kids."

One day Ian, who was then four, asked his mom if he could invite a friend to stay overnight. As parents do, Gail called the mother of the child to make the arrangements. The answer was a polite but definitive No!

Gail hung up the phone and called Ian over.

"Listen honey," she said. "Curtis cannot come over to spend the night. In fact, he cannot come over at all. His mom explained to me that he has only one lung and she is very careful not to expose him to any chance of cigarette smoke or anything else that would pose a threat to his health." At first Ian had a blank look on his face, till the message was fully understood. Then Niagara Falls started.

"The tears from Ian's face continued for three days. He just couldn't understand why I couldn't quit. Looking back, I am sure I probably had a few tears too," Gail explained. "It was one of those damned if you do, damned if you don't situations.

"You know you can do a lot for your kids to show them you love them. Most require large blocks of time, and a lot of it seems to require money. There are sacrifices and compromises, for sure. And, to be honest, sometimes there's resentment with these decisions. Any honest parent will tell you so. In this case, there was none of that. I had simply brotim my son's heart. Brotim hearts are mended with love. I knew there was only one thing to do. I had to quit smoking."

Smoking cessation for Gail was not an overnight process. It took several stressful weeks. As any of us can attest, to change habits just for ourselves is hard. Doing it for someone else doesn't make it any easier. But when our actions are motivated by love—for those we love—then we gain footing on a new level. With a good month behind her of smoke-free lungs, Gail made another phone call to Curtis' mom. This time she got the green light. Ian was beaming.

In simplest terms, compassion in action is an act of service. Until love is acted upon, it is merely a theory, a seed set upon inhospitable rocks. Fear is the motivating factor of stress. It undermines much of our behaviors. Compassion in action is a conscious act of love. We do acts of service not to make friends, to win brownie points, or earn favors from God. When we engage in acts of service, everyone benefits.

> Compassion in action is nothing less than an act of unconditional love. When we give in the name of service, we give to ourselves as well.

section four

Good Vibrations: Healing Techniques

A CONSENSUS AMONG THOSE AT THE VANGUARD of health suggests that Réne ("I think, therefore I am") Descartes was wrong. Mind and body are not two separate entities; they are one. Although Western science isn't quite sure exactly what the mind really is, this we do know: it's *not* the same thing as the brain. The mind merely uses the brain to function.

Our current understanding suggests that mind, or consciousness, in all its wonder appears to have an energy component to it. The laws of physics suggest that energy has vibrations. Bad energy is characterized by what is termed dissonance. Unresolved anger or fear are examples of bad energy. Good energy has resonance, harmony, syncopation. Love, joy, and happiness connote good energy. Light, sound, food, imagery, and breath are also forms of energy. With regard to effective stress management, each has the ability to heal or make whole. In simple terms, good vibrations bring a greater sense of inner peace, which after all, is what we strive for in this hectic pace of life, right?

Prolonged stress can have serious effects on the physical body, ranging from the common cold to cancer. Denied the chance to completely relax, one or more organs or physiological systems will show signs of dysfunction. This is why the regular practice of relaxation techniques is so important. These techniques allow the body to return to a sense of inner peace. In doing so, they help maintain the integrity of all the body's organs and systems. There are hundreds of relaxation techniques—from music therapy and physical exercise to hatha yoga, meditation, and t'ai chi. No one technique is better than the rest. It comes down to a matter of personal preference and time. The purpose of each technique is to calm body and mind, and this is where real healing takes place.

The following stories explore the nature of relaxation and restoring the body to wholeness through a host of various mind-body relaxation techniques that can best be described as "good vibrations."

1

The Sound of Music

Sound is energy made audible. Music is sound transformed. Some say that when we listen to music, we eavesdrop on the thoughts of God. Most people agree that music has a spiritual quality. Music is a gift from God, or so Orpheus thought. Greek legend has it that Orpheus was given a lyre by Apollo, the God of Music, so that he might offer songs of praise. Although Apollo bequeathed this gift, it was the Muses who taught Orpheus to play, hence the word "music." You don't have to understand the intricacies of tone, pitch, harmony, timbre, or rhythm to appreciate good vibrations. The sound of music has a healing quality which can motivate as well as pacify our deepest emotions.

Sound healing seems to work at many levels. First, there is the concept of entrainment, the sympathetic resonance of vibrations, which allows for a harmony between the vibration of music and the vibrations of cell tissue. Second, the ear structure is positioned near a lymph node, allowing a unique interaction with the immune system. Finally, through our perceptions music can heighten our enjoyment of the sounds we hear, resulting in a release of neuropeptides throughout the body, which also have a profound healing effect. Perhaps it's no surprise that a research study conducted by the Mitchum Corporation showed that listening to music was the number one relaxation technique used by thousands of people to calm their nerves.

Some listen to music, others play it. Recently I was moved by a story of the lead singer/fiddler Mairead Ni Mhaonaigh of the Irish group Altan. She and her husband Frankie Kennedy formed the group in 1986. Frankie died of cancer in 1992. It was his wish that the group continue on. And it has, with great success.

"The music was a healing force then," Mairead explained in an interview in the *Boulder Daily Camera*. "It lifted my spirits when things were low. When [Frankie] actually succumbed to cancer, the music was the only way to express those feelings."

I happened to see Altan perform some months after Frankie's death. Mairead has the most genuine smile and a calm presence. When she placed bow to fiddle, she became electric. It was no secret that music was and still is her healing force. She wasn't the only one who benefited, however—the audience did as well.

The sound of applause is not usually considered to be a symphony of sorts, but it is music to the ears of singer/songwriter Naomi Judd who, with her daughter Wynonna, formed one of the nation's most popular Country-Western music acts, The Judds. Stricken with a potentially fatal case of Hepatitis C in summer 1990, Naomi's singing career was nearly cut short. Told she might only have a few years to live, she was advised to prepare to die and sent home by her team of physicians. A woman of great faith, Naomi decided to listen to the voice in her heart, rather than those of her physicians. She resolved that she would not be a passive victim to her condition but would become an active participant in her own healing journey.

A longtime advocate of the mind-body-spirit connection, Naomi began to apply what she knew in her heart to be true. Setting her focus on healing, she planned a strategy for her recovery. One day after calling her husband Larry, her daughters Wynonna and Ashley, and her mom to her bedside, she informed them of her game plan. In her heart, Naomi knew that if she were to disconnect from her profession, her colleagues, and her music, she would die in record time.

Naomi decided to fight back. She announced to those around her that she would go back on tour, in what soon became known as "The Farewell Tour." But this was to be no ordinary tour. Not only would Naomi give the gift of music, this time she would receive it as well. Knowing how powerful the energy of love was, after performing each song she soaked up the applause, the whistles and the cheers, and directed this sonic energy throughout her body—asking the vibrations to stimulate her immune system, to heal the cells of her liver, and to send the virus into remission. In her own words, she said, "I would turn each standing ovation, this applause, into prayerful support."

And it worked! Nine years later, Naomi Judd is the picture of health. She makes no bones about sharing the message of faith, hope, and love—with a little music thrown in—as essential components of the mind-body-spirit equation.

In 1996, Naomi invited me to join her as a speaker on a panel at the National Wellness Conference in Stevens Point, Wisconsin. As panel moderator, Naomi asked me to speak of human spirituality as an integral part of the healing process. I cannot recall if music therapy entered the conversation that day, but it would certainly have fit in nicely.

Two years later, I was a guest at Naomi's annual celebrity auction in Nashville to raise research funds for the American Liver Foundation, of which she is the National Spokesperson. It was there I heard her say that for the past two years she has tested negative for the Hep C virus. Complete remission of Hep C is virtually unheard of, but Naomi just winked. She knows what it took to get there—good vibrations of all kinds.

Music has always held a soft spot in Naomi's heart and that spot continues to grow as she shares her message of the healing journey that we all must take part in to nurture our souls and become whole.

> Medicinal therapies are available in a great many ways. Music not only soothes the savage breast, it brings peace to the heart and soul as well.

2

When the Pupil Is Ready...

Joan has been meditating for years, but not long after she began to practice Insight Meditation, a technique she learned from Jon Kabat-Zinn, director of the Stress Reduction Clinic at the University of Massachusetts Medical Center, an insight came to her that had been waiting to be revealed and resolved for decades.

Meditation is a practice of cleansing the mind. Although it is often thought of as a religious practice, the premise of meditation is nondenominational and increasingly it is being used in the West as a stress-reduction technique. In fact, the American Heart Association now advocates meditation as stress prevention for coronary heart disease.

Meditation is increased concentration leading toward increased awareness. The purpose of meditation is to still the mind and quiet the voice of the ego, so that a sense of inner peace may permeate our being, bringing peace to the body as well. Mental homeostasis promotes physical homeostasis: decreased resting heart rate, blood pressure, muscle tension, and metabolic function. Meditation is not only good for the mind but wonderful for the body as well. When the mental chatter is stilled, unresolved issues residing fathoms below the conscious mind often bubble up to the surface, uncensored, where they may be reconciled.

One day, Joan was in such a relaxed state. Up to the surface came a voice, "You didn't save me!" Following the instructions she was taught, Joan took a deep breath and tried to dismiss this thought, as she had the others before it. But twice more she heard the same voice, bearing the same message. It took several moments for Joan to pull the pieces together, traveling back seventeen years to reconstruct the memory.

The year was 1980. Joan had completed nursing school in Chicago with a specialty in intensive critical care, coupled with a very short term in the Dominican Republic performing rural health care. This became the stepping-stone to her next assignment that same year—as a nurse in the American Refugee Center acute care hospital unit at Khao-I-Dang, Thailand. Across the boarder from Thailand lay the killing fields of Cambodia. Looming within earshot were Vietnamese troops, poised to attack. As Joan will tell you, this was not a re-creation of the television series *M*A*S*H:* "We, the Americans, had Hospital One. Across from us was the German Red Cross; down the row were the French, the English, and the Japanese. Our hospital was one large open room with about 100 plywood platform beds. It was always crowded with medical staff, assistants, translators, patients, their families, and visitors."

One afternoon, Joan was asked by a physician named Bob to escort a female patient across camp for a chest x-ray. The woman was diagnosed with Chinese Liver Fluke Disease. One look told Joan this woman was in serious pain. Her abdomen was grossly distended, stretched tight with fluid, ready to burst. Most likely she had contracted the disease from unfiltered water. It struck Joan as odd that this woman had traveled safely over a hundred miles of landmines to find shelter at the Thai border, only to succumb to this. The disease was quite advanced, but with her labored breathing, the physician wanted to see if it had progressed to her lungs. The best they could do was treat the symptoms and minimize the pain.

The woman was transported from a cot to a gurney to the back of dusty pick-up truck. As the vehicle pulled away, Joan saw three young girls run behind to catch up with their mother. From the young faces she turned to view the refugee living quarters; over 240,000 Cambodian, Vietnamese, and Chinese refuges cramped in a two-by-two-mile perimeter. Returning her glance inside the truck, Joan wiped her patient's brow and tried her best to keep the flies away from her face.

"I prayed that she would not die en route," Joan said. "I tried a couple of Hail Marys. I prayed, 'Mary, please don't let this woman die now. Not in the middle of camp, not with me along to attend to her, and especially not with her children watching.' But I was in Khao-I-Dang, Buddha's territory, and he is a brutal realist. His miracles are performed through insight, not some miraculous recovery."

The patient's breathing slowed considerably. Joan weighed her options. No crash cart, no ambulatory bags, no medical team, nothing! Was CPR even an option? Suddenly it was too late. The woman died. The annoying flies landed repeatedly on the corpse, as her three children, now orphaned, looked on with unyielding eyes.

"Back at the hospital, after seeing how upset I was, Dr.

Bob and the rest of the team calmly assured me that I had done the 'right thing.' But I was still plagued with questions. Had I played God? Had I made the wrong decision? If I had done CPR, how much longer would she have lived? Had I failed in my role to save and respond? Did I for one minute have the power to give the breath of life and refuse it? I wondered if her spirit lingered or did she move swiftly toward the light to welcome the pure freedom of breath without pain?" These questions remained unanswered in Joan's mind for seventeen years.

There is a Chinese proverb that states, "When the pupil is ready, the teacher will come." It refers to the idea that when we quiet our minds, become very still, wisdom rises from the depths of our unconscious mind to offer insight and illumination. We are then both student and teacher. Knowing this, sitting quietly, concentrating on her breath, Joan awaited the voice of the teacher. It said, "All breath moves toward wholeness."

Again came the woman's voice, "You did not save me." This time Joan answered, "No, I did not save you. I could not save you." Joan took several more slow deep breaths; the teacher spoke once more, "How does it feel not to have control? How does it feel to let go?"

Remember: When the pupil is ready, the teacher will come.

3

The Healing Power of Nature

Elizabeth Roberts is a most extraordinary woman. A teacher, philosopher, humanitarian, and social activist, Elizabeth is no stranger to the vanguard of social change. In the early '60s, she marched with the Reverend Martin Luther King Jr. to promote civil rights. Years later she launched a crusade for television reform. Her resume lists her as a former program director for National Public Radio, and it was she who coined the title for the now well-known afternoon news program "All Things Considered."

"Most likely that will be my epitaph," Elizabeth says, jokingly. Her most lasting legacy, however, may be her awareness of the healing power of nature.

I had been given her book *Earth Prayers* in 1992 by a very dear friend of mine in Vermont. So moved was I by the prayers and poems in this collection that I began to use several of them in a relaxation slide show I produced entitled, "Mother Gaia: The Healing Power of Nature." Word circulated about the tremendous impact of the slide show and one day I received a phone call from a conference coordinator wishing to team up Elizabeth and myself to do a joint presentation, with Elizabeth reciting the poems from her book. As it turned out, we both live in the same town, so we arranged to meet at her house one afternoon. Over a cup of tea she shared this story:

"How did the book come about?" she said, repeating my inquiry. "Let me tell you. I had been sick for quite some time with Chronic Fatigue Syndrome. It got so bad that I was bedridden for about nine months. It was horrible. I was so exhausted I could barely lift my hand up to my face. About the only thing I could do was read, but I was too tired to hold a book. The most I could hold up was a piece of paper.

"While I was sick, I had many conversations with God, many times not believing in a God anymore. My theology became a cosmology as I turned to the earth for help. And I got it.

"Elias, my husband, had sent the word out to my friends not to call because I couldn't hold the phone to talk. 'Instead,' he said to them, 'write letters.' So they did. Knowing how much I loved poetry, and knowing my love of nature, several friends sent me poems to read. In nine months' time I had quite a collection."

Elizabeth explained how her dark night of the soul became a womb of creation. She decided to edit the collection of poems into a book. *Earth Prayers* became her raison d'être and the energy to edit the collection became a healing energy itself. "Elias and I sent out invitations for our friends to contribute poems as well. And oh, the permissions to use some of these poems—you should see the folders in my office!" she exclaimed.

Through her illness, Elizabeth came to see what a powerful metaphor nature is. "Nature speaks to us in seasons. There is a time to produce and a time to lie fallow. In hindsight, I saw my downtime as that which my body needed to heal. Although I knew of the concept of lying fallow, it took Chronic Fatigue to make me realize I was not honoring this aspect of life. Now I have learned my lesson."

In 1990, Elizabeth and Elias formed The Boulder Institute for Nature and the Human Spirit, a social activist organization which promotes grassroots ecological projects as well as small-group vision quests in the quiet surroundings of Colorado's southwest corner. When Elizabeth speaks about the vision quests, her whole face lights up. "We have so much to learn from nature. Nature in all her infinite glory speaks to us, and we must listen."

Elizabeth is a person who walks her talk. It is not uncommon for her to be found responding to nature in a vision quest. She listens to the wisdom of the rocks, the songs of the trees, the lullabies of the streams, and the energies of the earth. And if you hike any of the many trails in Boulder's park system, you might well see Elizabeth out there. She partakes regularly in the healing process of nature. Her example is one to follow, for in this high-tech age it is all too easy to distance ourselves from our primal environment and lose contact with the heartbeat and resonance of Mother Nature.

> There is a right time for everything. A time to be quiet and a time to speak up, a time for keeping and a time for throwing away (Ecclesiastes: 3). May we often reconnect with the rhythms and healing energies of nature.

4

Inherit the Earth

One day over lunch, Elizabeth Roberts and her husband Elias shared with me a new book project they were working on.

"Have you noticed how much gloom and doom there is with the coming millennium?" Elias asked me. "We are inviting several hundred people to write prayers, poems, and messages for the new millennium. It is our hope that these prayers will be read throughout the world to create a critical mass of conscious thought and pull humanity in a positive direction.

"We want to get a message to the world's people that there is hope, that there is faith, to get us through the crises looming over our heads. You know, we are not going to make it if our only attitude is despair. We have contacted the Dalai Lama, Vaclav Havel, Joan Baez, Jane Goodall, Jimmy Carter, Thich Nhat Hanh, Desmond Tutu, and several others."

"Wow," I said, "this will be an impressive work." Reflecting on their two anthologies of collected poems and prayers, I felt this work would be a positive statement.

"Are you going to have any letters from children and young kids, perhaps even college students?" I asked.

"Oh," said Elizabeth, "that's right. We need the voice of children as well. Perhaps that can be its own chapter?"

Elias then turned to me and said, "Here. We'd like you to write one too. This is your formal invitation."

In my hands Elias placed a letter with the heading, "Prayers for 1000 Years: Invocations for the New Millennium." I was honored.

For well over a week I pondered what I would say to the people of tomorrow about the earth, about love, and about community. Hundreds of ideas circled in my mind. I continually asked myself, what message could I leave that would make a difference?

While it's true that children have an innate talent to live in the present moment, it would be unwise to think that today's younger generation lives a stress-free life. To the contrary, both children and teenagers face stressors similar to their parents' and grandparents'. And while the problems of youth may seem trivial compared to adult "real world" stressors, feelings of pain, fear, frustration, anxiety, and depression are identical to those of their grown-up counterparts. At some level, kids are quicker to adapt to the quickening speed of change in the world they stand ready to inherit; yet at another, bombarded with pessimistic headlines and newscasts, they too face the ever-present reality of global pollution, ethnic conflict, refugee migration, and financial crises, to name just a few foreseeable problems. However, if there is one attribute the youth of every age have, it is resiliency—the ability to bounce back.

Resiliency is a unique spiritual muscle. Like a special

flower, it is a hybrid of several coping skills which combine to overcome the winds of change, the odds against us. The fibers of resiliency are humor, creativity, persistence, and optimism, and their roots reach well below the surface, ready to rise again and again when needed. Perhaps its greatest facet is the ability to stay focused in the present moment, rather than stuck in the past or focused on the future. We enhance our resiliency when we galvanize these resources in the face of adversity. Each time we rise from the metaphorical fall, we come back stronger: what was once considered a mountain now becomes a molehill.

A week after meeting with Elizabeth and Elias, I sat in a restaurant in Boulder after a long hike in the mountains. For me, as for Elizabeth, the mountains always serve as a point of inspiration. I ordered my food and pulled out my notebook, ready to start my poem/prayer. No sooner did I put pen to paper than three high school kids came into the restaurant and were seated across from my table. I had momentarily forgotten that these kids were the audience for this book. My concentration was interrupted by the commotion and I placed my pen on the table. What initially started as a distraction became an inspiration, as I eavesdropped on their conversation. Here is the poem that came of that experience:

Inherit the Earth

I overheard a conversation among three teenagers yesterday.
They were discussing crime, pollution, and human values,
particularly the work ethic.
"The system appears to be corrupt," said one.

"Perhaps Earth is a prison and we are stuck here
until we wake up," said a second.
The third just shook her head in disgust.
This thought came to my mind:
It is said that the meek shall inherit the earth.
But after all we have done to it, will they still want it?
Soon, their conversation turned to giggles and laughter.
The energy shifted as did the topic, then more laughter.
In their mirth I heard defiance, resiliency, and faith.
Laughter, like hope, springs eternal.

5

The Body Flame

As a professor, I discovered that life in academia is comprised of three parts teaching, four parts research, and one part service to the community. For students, the academic life consists of three parts studying, eight parts partying, and four parts stress (usually from partying too much and studying too little). So part of my service to the community was to go to the residence halls during the most stressful times (such as during midterms and final exams), and teach relaxation techniques.

Most evening sessions were similar. A receptionist would meet me at the front desk and take me to the floor where the students were to congregate. I would walk into the lounge area and greet everybody. At the appointed time, somebody (usually the Resident Assistant) would formally introduce me to the crowd, and we would then form a circle on the carpeted floor. I would give a quick ten-minute presentation on the merits of relaxation during times of stress. At this point, I would invite the students to lie down on the floor and participate in a twenty-minute session of various relaxation techniques.

There are literally hundreds of techniques to promote relaxation, many of which fall into the category of mental imagery and visualization. After beginning each session with some diaphragmatic breathing, I would lead the group through a host of imagery exercises and close with some positive affirmation statements. Although the format was consistent from event to event, I would vary the imagery exercises, usually doing whatever came to mind that particular session.

One fall evening I shared with the group an exercise I call the Body Flame. In this particular visualization, you picture an image of a flame hovering above the center of your body (about an inch or two below your navel). The flame represents your body's stress level. A high torch-like flame is symbolic of a high stress level, while a small flame, like the pilot light of a gas stove, represents a state of relaxation. During this exercise, participants are encouraged to allow random thoughts, excess energy, and toxic emotions to pass from the mind to the stomach and up through the flame where they would be burned off, returning the mind-body to a greater state of homeostasis.

Throughout the exercise, I would gently remind students to take a comfortably deep breath, concentrate on the image of the flame (its color, size, shape, and movement), and ask them to continually send any thoughts and feelings that were no longer needed to fuel the Body Flame. Toward the end, I would invite the students to imagine their body flame as low-maintenance flame, indicative of a state of tranquility. Perhaps because of the anticipated stress from their looming exams, the students were quite receptive to this exercise.

When the lights came back up one particular evening,

I was greeted with the smiles and relaxed faces of those students now ready to return to their books. One fellow, a young man with deep black eyes, walked up to me, shook my hand, and told me this was the most profound experience he had ever had. He thanked me profusely, then, slowly turning toward the door, gave me an authentic salute and walked away. I stayed to chit-chat with the remaining students who hung around. When everyone had left, I walked to my car and drove home.

About a year later, I was asked back to the same dorm. Again I began the session with some diaphragmatic breathing and then slipped into a visualization exercise I call the Rainbow Meditation, matching each color of the rainbow with a specific body region. When the meditation exercise was over, the lights came back up and students slowly made their way back to their rooms. As usual, I hung around to chat with students and then picked up my things to go home. In the corner of the lounge stood a young man with black hair, a goatee, and deep black eyes. He waited until the crowd had left and then approached me, extending his right hand.

"Great session, Dr. Seaward," he said. "I really enjoyed it, but you didn't do the Body Flame this time. How come?"

Not recognizing him at first, I was caught off-guard by the question.

"Well, there are so many mental imagery exercises, I just do whatever comes to mind," I answered. As I looked into his eyes, I remembered our encounter the previous year.

"I was hoping you'd do it again." he said. "You see, I have been doing that particular exercise every day on my own since I learned it from you. Several years ago I was diagnosed with a severe stomach ulcer. The medications have been as bad as the problem itself. That first night, when you talked us through the visualization, I placed the body flame over my stomach, and it was the first time I felt complete relief. I am happy to say that within three months, the ulcer disappeared. I am off medication and I feel great. Thanks!"

This technique is really quite simple—and useful. Here's how to do it:

1. First, lie down with your arms comfortably at your side. Try to keep your spine aligned from your head to your hips. Gently close your eyes and focus your attention on your breathing. Feel the air come into your nose and mouth and down into your lungs, and as you do this, feel your stomach rise up, then descend back down as the air begins to leave through your mouth. Make each breath comfortably deep and relaxed.
2. Now, with your eyes closed, try to locate the center of your body, your center of gravity. If you are like most people, it will be about an inch or two below your navel. Place your attention there just so you are aware of this body region.
3. Next, imagine a flame hovering over that point, the center of your body. Metaphorically speaking, this flame is a symbol of your state of relaxation. It feeds off your body's energy. When the body has an abundance of energy—nervous or negative energy—this flame will be quite tall, perhaps even like a blowtorch. When you are completely

relaxed, the flame will be quite small. I call this a "maintenance flame," like a pilot light in a gas stove.

4. Using your mind's eye, imagine the size of your flame. See its size relative to your body's level of energy. What color is your flame? Is it an intense brilliant yellow-white? Now look at its shape. Is the bottom round or oval-shaped? What does your flame look like? As you look toward the top of the flame, you will see it comes to a jagged point. Your flame may even dance around a bit. As you look at this flame, feel it feed off the excess energy in your body. Let your flame burn off any excess energy you feel may be detracting from your ability to relax. If you happen to have any wandering thoughts which pull your attention away from the image of the flame, try to send these up through the flame and redirect your thoughts back to this image. With each breath you take, allow any excess energy or draining thoughts to move from your head down to your stomach and become fuel for the body's flame. In doing so, you release the tension in your mind and body and become more relaxed.

5. As you continue to watch the image of the flame, feel your body slowly become calm and relaxed. As your body becomes tranquil, notice the flame decrease in height. Soon you will notice that your flame is decreasing in size, to only about a quarter- to a half-inch tall. Continue to notice the color, shape, and size of the flame. Feel your body relax even more as your attention is affixed to this

image. Continue to keep your mind's eye focused on your body flame.

6. When you feel completely relaxed, with your flame very small, very still, allow the image to fade from your mind, but retain the feeling of relaxation.

> The mind and body work as one entity in the healing process. As we release excess or toxic thoughts that no longer serve us, we bring the body back to a greater sense of relaxation and restored health.

6

Dreams Revisited

In fall 1986, I was invited to become a member of the sports medicine council of the U.S. Olympic Biathlon Team. Biathlon is a winter sport that combines cross-country skiing with rifle marksmanship. The sport evolved from the practice of winter hunting in the Scandinavian countries. Europeans were genetically programmed for this sport, with over a thousand years of practice to brag about. We Americans, on the other hand, have only about twenty years' collective practice under our belts. To be honest, our team needed a lot of help.

The financial windfall of the 1984 Los Angeles Olympics trickled down into the coffers of each sport. While some teams bankrolled their million-dollar booty, the Biathlon team chose to spend it, in hope of earning the ever-elusive Gold Medal for their sport. An elite coach was hired from Norway, and a council was formed to offer the best sports medicine services our athletes could receive.

My job was to introduce and integrate several aspects of mental training, primarily skills to promote relaxation. During various training camps, I would fly in and set up shop in the hotel. My routine went like this: I would put a sign-up sheet on my hotel door with hourlong slots for sports psych sessions. Athletes would come into my room, sit and talk for a few minutes about the various stresses of amateur athletics, then lie down on a bed and be taken through a series of relaxation exercises.

On a trip to Lake Placid, New York, where the team often trained, I arrived at the hotel and, after I had settled in, placed a sign-up sheet outside my door—open for business. On the second day, I walked back to my room from lunch to find the coach's name penned in for the seven o'clock hour. Coaches are not exempt from stress, but I was a bit surprised, thinking that my responsibilities were solely to the athletes. At seven o'clock, Hans walked into my room, his characteristic gregarious smile absent.

In a thick Norwegian accent, he humbly asked, "Do you have time for me to come to you now?"

"Yes, please come in," I replied.

Hans approached the spare bed and sat down. Placing his hands to his eyes, he rubbed his face and sighed. He began to explain a recurring dream he had had for several weeks. It was obvious to me before he even began how disturbing its message was. In a dream state, Hans would return home to Norway to find two open coffins in the family room. In the first was the body of his wife, in the second lay his newborn daughter.

"What does it mean? Can you help me?" came his distraught voice.

In *Man and His Symbols,* Carl Gustav Jung spoke of recurring dreams. Dreams, Jung wrote, were the language of the unconscious mind. Dreams rich in color, symbolism, and meaning are meant to be explored, not ignored, in a conscious state. In particular, it was his opinion that recurring dreams were related to unfinished business of the soul. Jung proposed an exercise called "Active Imagination" in which a person in a relaxed lucid state could re-enter the dream and "finish the script," in effect completing the unfinished business, which in turn allows them to move on. By doing this, the dreamer begins the resolution process and, in most cases, episodes of the recurring dream cease. I myself have had great luck practicing Active Imagination to resolve a recurring dream I'd been having a few months earlier, involving a huge, black, ferocious dog. So to help Hans, I drew upon Jung's wisdom for my answer.

"Let's try something, Hans," I said. "Let's recreate the dream right now, but let's finish it. Lie down and get as relaxed as you can. Take a few deep breaths. I am going to share some images with you. Use your imagination to make these images as real for you as possible. Embellish them with rich detail to make the image as real as possible."

Once Hans appeared relaxed, I described the scene in his family room as he described it to me. After having him take a slow, deep breath, I invited Hans to imagine that the coffins were transformed into a really large bed. I asked Hans to approach the bed, lie down next to his daughter and wife, cuddle with them, and feel the warmth of their skin.

"Listen to the rhythmic sounds of their breath," I said. "Your wife and child are very much alive, just sleeping, waiting for your return."

Next, I invited Hans to speak softly to his wife, telling her he was home for an extended time now, telling her that he loved her, how much he missed her, and how glad he was to see her and their daughter.

"All is well," I said, "All is well."

Within moments, Hans appeared completely at ease. He slowly opened his eyes and smiled. Something inside him had changed. He thanked me, rose to his feet, and said he had to make a phone call.

The next morning at the breakfast table Hans came up behind me, placed his large hands on my neck and began to massage my shoulders.

"I had the best night sleep in two months," he began. "You work miracles! I called my wife early this morning; we had been out of touch for several weeks. Everything is OK now," he said, slapping me on the back and laughing. Then he turned to the six Olympians and said in Norwegian, "*Ardi Fardi!*"—"Let's go!"

> Carl Jung once said, "The dream is a little hidden door into the innermost and most secret recesses of the soul." If you listen and decode the message of your dream, stress will dissipate like a faded memory.

7

Curiosity and the CAT Scan

An ageless proverb reminds us that "curiosity killed the cat." I don't know cats well enough to comment, but from my experience as a teacher and therapist, I can say that curiosity is one of the more commonly used muscles of the soul in times of stress. And while too much of anything can be unhealthy, searching for answers to life's more threatening questions is considered by many to be an essential coping tool. Academically speaking, curiosity as an inner resource is termed "information seeking." When the red light of stress goes on, all senses are on alert for information on how to best get to safety.

So perhaps it came as no surprise when the phone rang at 6:00 A.M. sharp one Tuesday morning. A friend from the East Coast was already in high gear, seeking some indispensable information. Although I immediately recognized her voice, there was a peculiar dissonance coming through the line. Within seconds, Susan explained that a routine mammogram a day earlier led to a suspicious CAT scan. The diagnosis was breast cancer, and her physician suspected it had metastasized to her spine and lymph nodes as well. Susan said she was taking it well, but her voice was not convincing.

I had met Susan at a conference a few years earlier. A wellness director at a small New England college, she was attending a workshop I gave on mind-body-spirit healing. Sitting in a circle with fellow participants, Susan, like many others, was taking copious notes as a strategy to incorporate the information into her own campus wellness program. At the time, she confided, the material presented was purely theoretical. Now Susan wanted 100 percent application.

"Luke, can you help me design a healing program? I am open to anything," she said, bringing calmness to her voice.

"Sure," I replied. "Let's see," I stalled, staring into the darkness, as I composed my thoughts. "OK, got paper and a pen? Here we go."

Drawing on the wellness model of healing that I learned from Dr. Elizabeth Kübler-Ross, I sketched out a list of ideas, suggestions, and recommendations, and gave her some local contacts in her area. The healing template covered everything from nutrition and mental imagery to acupuncture, music therapy, affirmations, prayer, and a "healing Treasure Map." Susan was all ears and she repeated, with great frequency, my comments to make sure she had heard every word correctly.

"Just a minute," she said, "I'm writing everything down, let me hear it again."

Her behavior was far from unique. Canceled air flights, stock market fluctuations, or midterm exams can all activate the curiosity antenna. In my opinion, however, cancer (or any life-threatening diagnosis) pushes the button with the greatest force. "How did I get it?" and "How do I get rid of it?" are typically the first two questions asked. After a few hours on the phone, Susan's voice sounded much better, and heartfelt laughter had replaced the nervous giggles I heard earlier in the conversation. "I'm going to bounce back from this, I just know it," she said confidently.

Two days later, I learned that Susan's lumpectomy occurred without incident, but the bone marrow transplant had her a little more concerned. She was scheduled to fly to Houston in a few months. She was told by her physician to use the interim time to regain her full strength. To Susan this meant not only physical strength but mental, emotional, and spiritual fortitude as well. She promised she would keep me updated regularly on her progress.

In addition to her chemotherapy and radiation, Susan pulled together many different resources to create her own personal holistic healing program. Here is the template of her healing process. (Please note: these suggestions are drawn from a specific case, and it would be to your advantage to include the involvement of your physician in designing a program for yourself, just as Susan did. However, if your physician is not open to holistic healing practices, you do have a right to change physicians. It is important to have a doctor on board whose health philosophy is similar to your own.)

This template of ideas and recommendations comes from my mind-body-spirit healing workshop and is considered to be a stepping-stone to optimal health. As you will see, most if not all of these recommendations either directly or indirectly affect the efficiency of your immune system. The standard holistic approach involves the four components of optimal well-being: body, mind, emotions, and spirit. Let's start with the body, since it is the most tangible of the four.

Physical Well-Being

Good nutrition is essential for good health. Today there are hundreds of synthetic substances in our food to preserve shelf-life and enhance corporate profits. In simple terms, these substances are toxic to the body's physiology. The American Cancer Society states that from 40 to 50 percent of cancers are the result of a poor diet. Hippocrates, the father of modern medicine, who said "First, do no harm," also said, "Let food be your medicine and medicine be your food." Great advice! So here we go:

1. Eat a large amount and variety of vegetables, preferably at midday and evening meals. Veggies are said to have phytonutrients which help boost the immune system. Soy products have phytoestrogens which are thought to be very helpful for women with breast cancer. Fresh organic veggies contain more nutrients (vitamins and minerals) than canned or frozen veggies. They also contain fiber which is thought to reduce the risk of colon cancer, and possibly remove toxins from other foods that might enter the bloodstream. Fruits are good; however, cancer cells thrive on foods with high sugar content so, eat fruit in moderation. Fresh, local, organically grown fruits are considered the best source.

2. Consume good sources of vitamins and minerals. Vitamins A (beta carotene) C, and E are antioxidants which help fight free radicals and boost the immune system. The best source of vitamins is a natural source, not synthetic. Also, do a test on your vitamins to see if they really are bioavailable to healthy cells in your body. Some products are synthesized with insoluble binders, making them pass completely through your gastrointestinal track undigested and unabsorbed, resulting in expensive urine. To test your vitamin, place a tablet in an eight-ounce glass of water with one teaspoon of vinegar. If it does not dissolve in twenty minutes, find a brand that does.
3. Eat foods that are whole and natural. Avoid highly processed foods, especially foods that contain hydrogenated oils or partially hydrogenated oils (for example, many commercial baked goods, snacks, cereals, and the like). These contain trans-fatty acids that are toxic to cell tissue. And it's not a bad idea to cut down on your consumption of fats; an increased consumption of fat is thought to decrease the efficiency of your immune system. The more processed food you eat, the harder your immune system has to work to clean up the toxins. As Andy Weil, M.D., states in his book *Spontaneous Healing,* this is energy better spent on working to dismantle cancerous tumors. Eating whole organic (pesticide-free, hormone-free, herbicide-free) foods allows the immune system to attend to areas in greater need.

4. Reduce your consumption of dairy products. Today's milk is far different than it was years ago. Most commercially produced milk contains hormones, pesticides, herbicides, and antibiotics in doses which, over time, significantly weaken the immune system. The same holds true for ice cream, butter, and cheese. Where you can, buy organic dairy products. If these are not available, try mixing rice milk with your milk to cut down on the level of toxins. For a change, try almond cheese and yogurt, a great source of nutrients.

   The American diet is extremely low in essential fatty acids, those which the body cannot produce and must acquire from outside sources. The essential fatty acids are Linolenic (Omega 3), which is found in cold-water fish such as salmon, tuna, trout, etc., and flax seed oil; and Linoleic (Omega 6), found in nuts, safflower oil, corn oil, canola oil, and eggs. Not only is there a dearth of Omega 3 in our diet, but the imbalance of Omega 3 to Omega 6 fatty acids is thought to be harmful as well. It would be an excellent idea to include a regular intake of Omega 3-rich foods.

5. Avoid artificial products such as MSG and Aspartame (Nutrasweet®), as these negatively affect the functioning of neurotransmitters in the brain. There have been more complaints about Aspartame to the Food and Drug Administration (FDA) in the past ten years than for all other food additives, but for political reasons nothing has been done. (Blaylock, *Excitotoxins*, 1994.)

6. Stop using the microwave oven. Microwaves employ ELF (extremely low frequency) vibrations, and these are known to increase the proliferation of cancer cells. (Becker, *Cross Currents*, 1990.)

7. Try acupuncture, specifically five-element classical acupuncture, where the practitioner takes pulses before inserting tiny needles. Five-element acupuncture is a holistic approach to wellness, not merely symptomatic relief. It is based on the ancient Chinese concept of the body's human energy field and meridian system. A good practitioner will have studied acupuncture in a reliable school for at least three to four years. Many physicians in the United States become eligible to practice by taking a two-week seminar and watching forty hours of videos; some physicians have no training whatsoever. So check your practitioner's credentials before you undergo acupuncture treatment. If you do not like your first session, find another practitioner. It's always a good idea to seek references.

8. Schedule regular full-body massages according to your schedule and budget. Actually, massage is just one of many different types of bodywork. But muscle tension is the number one symptom of stress, so getting a massage is a good place to start. Many types of bodywork include energy healing, such as Reiki, zero point balancing, Therapeutic Touch, Healing Touch, bio-energy, etc. Relatively new to Western culture, energy work is an ancient method of healing based on the premise that human beings are comprised of layers of energy. It is based on the

idea that disease doesn't start in the body but only manifests itself there. Energy healing works with the immune system, which extends well beyond the physical body. If this is something you wish to explore, ask around for a good practitioner or call the office of the International Society for the study of Subtle Energy and Energy Medicine (ISSSEEM) and ask them if they can refer you to someone in your region (see the Resource Guide at the back of this book).

9. Physical exercise is part of living a balanced life. The regular secretion of the stress hormone cortisol is known to destroy white blood cells. Exercise utilizes cortisol, as well as other stress hormones such as epinephrine, norepinephrine, thyroxin, and aldosterone, thus helping to keep the body's physiology in balance. Research shows that lack of exercise tips the hormonal scale out of favor of an enhanced immune system. Regular rhythmic exercise (such as brisk walking), for as little as twenty minutes a day, helps restore this balance.
10. Get adequate amounts of full-spectrum sunlight (about twenty minutes per day). Light is an essential nutrient. Today most people don't get an adequate supply of full-spectrum sunlight. You don't need much, but you do need some, every day if possible.
11. Drink chemicalfree-water. Tap water has lots of chemicals, including chlorine and floride. Although they are used to keep water clean, they are not without problems. Filtered water is great

but essential minerals may also be filtered out, so be sure these are replenished. Bottled water is good, but there are no FDA regulations on bottled water, so ask lots of questions at the health food store. Drinking plenty of good water helps aid the detoxification process of your body.

12. There are many herbs that are good for healing. Try to find a good source for herbal therapies. Several herbs help boost the immune system, including echinacea, goldenseal, and astragulus; however, there are caveats with each one (for example, echinacea should be taken only for short periods of time, not every day). Also, taking milk thistle to help cleanse the liver is a good idea. If you are using antibiotics, you may want to take supplementary acidophilus (good intestinal bacteria), which is destroyed in the small intestine through the use of antibiotics. This can lead to candida and again will compromise the immune system. For more information, purchase a good reference book or try calling the Herb Research Foundation (see Resource Guide).

13. Try to keep your sleeping, eating, and exercise habits on a regular schedule: have meals at regular scheduled times, always go to bed by 10:00 P.M., etc. The body responds well to a healthy twenty-four-hour cycle.

14. Allocate from ten to twenty minutes a day to some type of relaxation technique. During this period, allow yourself quiet time to relax and do absolutely nothing.

Emotional Well-Being

1. Creative Anger Management: There is a large aspect of grieving in the healing process, and the initial stages of grieving involve anger. Repressing anger may prolong the grieving process, thereby making you less emotionally healthy. First, realize that it is OK to be angry. Anger is a normal emotion; however it is most healthy in very small amounts. Suppressed anger can suppress the immune system and become toxic to the body. Venting anger is considered good when it is directed toward the aggressor, but sometimes just yelling at the sky helps, too. Set aside some time each day or each week to feel and creatively release your anger. A good book on anger management is Harriet Lerner's *The Dance of Anger.*

   Anger is also related to fear. If you are not feeling any sense of anger, check your fear barometer. Talking, writing, and acting out feelings of fear can be cathartic, helping relieve the accumulation of these toxic feelings.

2. Music Therapy: The body has a natural rhythm of about 7.8 hertzs (cycles per second). Healthy musical rhythms are said to entrain the body to a homeostatic level of 7.8 Hz. Not all music does this, however; classical music, some new age, and some (slow) jazz are best. Music with lyrics typically does not. Dolphin and whale music is said to be at 7.8 Hz, which is why you will find these types of sounds mixed in relaxing nature soundtracks. The bottom line is to find acoustic music

you like to relax to and let it do its thing. Music therapy can most certainly have an effect on your emotions, which is why personal preference is so important. Listening to music to relax is a great way to promote healing, but mixing your own tape of healing, upbeat music works as well. This can be played in the car or anywhere. Good sources of relaxing music (without lyrics) include Kay Gardner and Steven Halpern, and can be found in your local music store or special ordered. There is a lot of great music out there. Explore and have fun.

On another note, when you turn the stereo up, turn the television off (due to the proliferation of negative newscasts). Andy Weil, M.D., recommends taking a news "fast." I think this is an excellent idea. If there is something really important going on, trust that you will hear about it. Television has an addictive quality. Try to wean yourself off of it periodically.

3. Humor Therapy: Laughter is good medicine. Try building a humor library! Put out the search for funny audiotapes, books, movies, and videos—anything that will increase your humor quotient to a minimum twenty laughs per day. Expand your humor venues beyond television. Making a "tickler notebook" is a good idea: start collecting comics, photos, cards, poems, letters—anything that lifts your spirits. There is also a wonderful humor conference put on by Joel Goodman's The Humor Project (see Resource Guide).

Mental Well-Being

1. Mental Imagery and Visualization (healing images, etc.): Mental imagery and visualization are mental training techniques to harness the power of the mind to heal. Years of research suggests that it is best for each individual to come up with a personal healing image, rather than using one suggested by a therapist or counselor. This way the image you come up with is unique to you and, for this reason, works most powerfully. For instance, Susan used an image of her chemo drugs as gardeners who were helping her. Using mental imagery to aid drug therapy, radiation treatment, and surgery is a wonderful idea.

   Mental imagery can be done along with positive affirmations (see below) or it can be done while meditating. It can also be done several times in the course of a day as a simple reminder to keep your conscious and unconscious mind working together, rather than in opposition, which is often the case.

   Visualization is best described as a conscious choice with intention, whereas imagery can be defined as a spontaneous flow of thought originating from the unconscious mind toward consciousness. Pick an image which you find relaxing or healing and, using the imagination of your five senses, make the image as real and powerful as possible. Possible images for healing and relaxation are limitless.

2. Positive Affirmations: Think of a word or a phrase you can repeat to yourself many times a day. Some people even suggest writing it down fifteen times a day. Make it a simple phrase, and begin with the words *I am*...

   A positive affirmation statement should be *positive*—"I am healthy," not "I am not going to die," as this is interpreted unconsciously as "I am going to die." And a positive affirmation statement should always be stated in the present tense.

3. Art Therapy: The purpose of art therapy is to let the unconscious mind speak to the conscious mind while you're awake (as opposed to in a dream state). The unconscious mind uses the language of colors, shapes, and symbols. Everything you draw on paper has meaning. Even if you drop the crayon and it makes a mark, this has some meaning which hopefully will be revealed to you. It doesn't matter what your artistic ability is, whether you draw at the third-grade level or like Michalangelo. It makes no difference!

   Once you get a box of crayons or pastels and a pad of large paper, draw an image of your illness, what it seems like to you. Your image can be either symbolic or representational. For example, a cancerous tumor can be drawn like Casper the Friendly Ghost or like an actual cancerous tumor. White blood cells can appear like angels, white sharks, spaceships, or like scientific renderings of cells with a nucleus and cell membrane. Let your mind speak to you as to how to draw the image.

There are no wrong images.

After you draw the first image of how things are and how you feel, next draw an image of how you wish to be—the end result of your cancer. Drawing this image sends a strong message to your unconscious mind of your intention to orchestrate your health in this direction. Post the second picture on the fridge, bathroom mirror, or some place you can see it every day as a reminder of your optimal health goal.

4. Treasure Map: This is a fun exercise. Pull out about ten to twenty magazines on a variety of different topics. Next, get a large piece of paper (oak tag or newsprint), a pair of scissors, and a gluestick. Then start going through the collection of magazines looking for images, photographs, and words of healing (for example, organic vegetables, a flower garden, joggers on a beach, etc.). If you don't see specific words, cut out letters or print a word, phrase, or poem from a computer file.

   By collecting and arranging an assortment of images, photos, and words, you begin to work with the unconscious mind as well as the conscious mind to move in the direction of optimal health. The unconscious mind speaks a language rich in color, symbols, and images. When you are done, place your treasure map in a place where you can see it every day, often. The treasure map acts like a compass to guide your mind and you to inner peace.

Spiritual Well-Being

1. Prayer and Meditation: Regular conversations with God, however you conceive him/her/it to be, are always good. Talk to God. If you must, *yell* at God, ask questions. Make demands. Make *specific* demands. In her book *A Book of Angels*, Sophy Burnham describes the steps on how to pray. These steps are identical as those suggested for mental imagery and guided visualization. They include:

    - Honor the present moment: speak in the present tense.
    - Accentuate the positive: speak in a positive (not negative) light.
    - Send a clear transmission: focus and concentrate on your intentions.
    - Detach from the outcome.
    - Practice an attitude of gratitude. Give thanks.

    Meditation is a means to clear the mind. A clear mind promotes a clear body, as the two are really one. Take some time each day, as little as five minutes, to sit quietly with no interruptions. Allow the thoughts and feelings that come to mind to leave with each exhalation.

2. Journaling: Journaling is a great way to get thoughts and feelings down on paper. It can be very cathartic, which in itself is quite healthy. It is also a great way to do some soul-searching—the search for meaning and purpose. Start by getting a notebook dedicated just for this technique and make it confidential (for your eyes only). If a

blank piece of paper is too overwhelming, try picking up a book on journal writing. There are many good books and hundreds of themes on which to write. Knowing the importance of stories, perhaps one journal theme to start with is to write your own story.

3. Connections to Nature: A walk in the woods, an hour in a garden or at the beach are great ways to cleanse and renew the spirit. Get in touch with the seasons, the cycles of the moon, the oceanic tides, the migration patterns of regional birds, the names of trees—these are all part of our connection to nature. By getting out in nature, away from the hectic rush of life (telephones, e-mail, pagers, fax machines, radio and television) we begin to resonate with the healing energies of the planet and in turn, bring our mind-body-spirit back to a greater state of homeostasis.
4. Support Groups: Make a list of your friends and family. Who on this list is available to sit and talk, who will be there for you when you need someone to listen? If your list is short or skimpy, find a local support group of people with a similar background (gardeners, cancer patients, single parents, mystery book lovers, bungee-jumpers). If there is no group that matches your interests, start one and meet at least once a month.
5. Practice Forgiveness: Holistic healing means coming to a sense of inner peace. We can start by forgiving those we feel have done us wrong. Forgiveness also means forgiving ourselves for

> whatever injustices we may have done to friends, family, acquaintances, neighbors. The word *remission* has several meanings; one is forgiveness. It's something to think about.

As Susan soon found out, doing all these things to promote healing is nothing less than a full-time job. Too many behavioral changes made all at once can lead to a severe rebound effect. Try to modify your health behaviors accordingly. The best definition of optimal wellness I have come across is this: Optimal wellness is the integration, balance, and harmony of mind, body, spirit, and emotions. A good healing program honors the concept that the whole is greater than the sum of the parts; healing means coming to a greater sense of inner peace, not necessarily alleviating or reducing the symptoms of disease or illness. Ultimately, a holistic approach to healing is one in which you take responsibility for your healing process rather than giving your power away to medical staff or holistic care practitioners.

One Saturday morning several weeks after my first phone conversation with Susan, the phone rang again.

"I want to give you a progress report," she said, calmly. "First, I'm feeling much better. Second, the affirmations have helped a lot. Third, I have cut out all processed foods, transfatty acids, MSG, Aspartame, and I'm taking loads of antioxidants—I feel great! My support group is wonderful! I stopped using the microwave. I've started regular acupuncture sessions, and I go for long walks in the woods and talk with God. If the weather is bad, I sit in my room and pray."

"Let me tell you about my visualizations," she exclaimed joyfully. "I am on two drugs, Cytoxin and

Andromyosin. This may sound crazy, but I have assigned a cute old man to the first and a woman, his wife, to the second; they are Uncle Cy and Aunt Andri. They are gardeners and they help me by going through my body and weeding out the bad cells so the flowers and fruits can grow and bloom. Every day, several times a day, actually, I say hi to Uncle and Aunt, knowing full well they are busy at work and doing a great job. I feel great!"

"I made some goals, too. I've scheduled a trip to Europe about three months after the bone marrow transplant. I have always wanted to go to Europe! My doctor said it was OK. Say, what do you know about Italy and France? Ever been?"

When Norman Cousins rebounded, through the use of humor therapy, from a life-threatening disease, his premise of holistic healing was that each person must take responsibility for his or her own health. Susan has done just that, and her example reminds us to do the same.

8

The Story of Garrett Porter

Patricia Norris is a rare national treasure in the field of health promotion. Long before mind-body-spirit healing was given the name psychoneuroimmunology (PNI), Pat, a psychologist working at the Menniger Clinic in Topeka, Kansas, was engaged in the integration of mind, body, spirit, and emotions in the successful effort to promote healing in people with chronic diseases.

Pat comes from a family of scientists and practitioners in the allied health fields. Her mother, Alyce, and stepfather, Elmer Green, pioneered the work of biofeedback, making it a household word. Their explorations into human consciousness laid the groundwork for what is now known as PNI. "Growing up under the roof of two very curious-minded parents," Pat explains, "the concepts that influenced my childhood had much to do with mind-body unity."

She became fascinated with the research her parents were conducting on yogis from India who had what appeared to be uncanny control of various body functions, including their heart rate, ventilation, blood pressure, blood flow, and temperature regulation. Some could breathe less than once a minute—comfortably. Others could shift all the blood in their body to the right side, leaving the left stone-cold. This wasn't magic; it was incredible mind-body control. Western science was of the opinion that this aspect of human physiology was autonomic and that human thought had little or no influence over it. As her parents came to learn, the mind is not separate from the body but works in unison with it. Self-regulation is the term Pat likes to use when describing the mind-body link.

I first met Pat at a biofeedback conference in Colorado Springs in 1990. It was there I heard her tell the remarkable story of Garrett Porter.

In July 1978, at the age of nine, Garrett was diagnosed with an inoperable malignant brain tumor, an astrocytoma located in the right hemisphere of his brain. Although radiation therapy was used, it appeared to be ineffective and the cancerous tumor grew. The doctors gave Garrett less than a year to live. But Garrett refused to believe his death sentence. Never once did he choose anything but life. In an attempt to seek help, his parents sought the assistance of someone who understood the mind-body connection. Their trail led them to the door of Dr. Patricia Norris.

Pat met with Garrett and the two formed a bond of everlasting friendship. As her first cancer patient, Garrett was exposed to several different mind-body techniques. It was Pat's intention to create a program for Garrett similar to that designed by her colleague Carl Simonton. Garrett's weekly sessions consisted of a specially designed relaxation tape, mental imagery and visualization, some art therapy, and biofeedback. In only a matter of days, Pat knew she had someone special in Garrett, a little boy with a tremendous imagination and an incredible will to live.

One day, while doing a session of art therapy, Garrett drew his tumor as Planet Meatball and several white blood cells in the shape of Pacman, ready to devour it. Each white blood cell had a squiggly line. When Pat asked Garrett what that represented, he answered, "Aw, gee, Dr. Norris, don't you know? Those are antennas, that's how they talk to each other." Not until a few years later did neurophysiologist Candace Pert discover that the mind-body link is created through neuropeptides and a vibration which acts like an antenna for various cells to communicate to each other.

In October 1979, Garrett informed his father one night that he couldn't visualize his tumor, and he could only conclude that it was gone. All he could see in his visualization was a tiny white dot where the tumor had been. In a matter of months a CAT scan proved what Garrett already knew. In February 1980, clinical tests revealed no cancerous tumor; the doctor assumed Garrett had undergone surgery. In its place was a small calcium deposit—the small white dot Garrett saw in his visualization. Indeed, the tumor was gone.

For some, those who see, believe. For others, those who believe, see.

9

The Breath of Life

Approaches to managing stress are as varied as the people who use them. Perhaps due to the complexity of human nature and the daily events we find ourselves in, it is fair to say that no two people will deal with stress the same way. Yet if there were one relaxation technique that could be described as "one size fits all," belly-breathing would win hands down. The long deep sigh, the epitome of taking a moment to relax, is really what belly-breathing is all about. Unlike most techniques, it can be done anywhere at any time, and no one is the wiser.

Breathing is easy; we pretty much take it for granted because it doesn't require a whole lot of thought. But by and large Americans are chest-breathers (whether you are a man or a woman, I guess it looks good to have a big chest!). The problem with chest-breathing is that it places pressure on a bundle of nerves under the breastbone and can actually trigger the stress response. Of course, when we sleep the ego is off-duty and we revert back to belly-breathing—the style most conducive for relaxation.

Ancient mystics tell us that the words *breath* and *spirit* are synonymous, suggesting that divine energy is found within the precious movements of inhalation and exhalation. As such, the breath of life is no mere metaphor. Interestingly enough, every technique to promote relaxation employs some aspect of breathing and this is the technique I begin each class with. A wise sage once said, "There are forty different ways to breathe." Here are two styles I use in my classes.

Breathing Clouds

This technique can be traced back to the origins of Eastern philosophy and religion both in India, with the practice of yoga, and in Japan, with the practice of Zen meditation. It was introduced as a cleansing process for the mind and body, the end result being complete relaxation. You can do this technique either sitting or lying down.

To begin, close your eyes and focus all your attention on your breathing. Focus on drawing air from your belly. Try inhaling through your nose and exhaling through your mouth. Visualize the air that you breathe in as clean, fresh air, pure and energized air, like a white puffy cloud.

As you breathe in this clean, pure air, visualize and feel it enter your nose and circulate up through the sinus cavity to the top of your head, and down the back of your spinal column. As you end the inhalation, imagine the air circulating through your entire body.

Now, as you exhale, visualize that the air leaving your body is dirty, hazy air, which symbolizes all the stressors, frustrations, and toxins throughout your mind and body. With each breath you take, allow the clean, fresh air to enter and circulate and invigorate your body, while the expulsion of the dirty air helps rid your body of its stress and tension.

Repeat this breathing cycle for five to ten minutes. As you repeat the "breathing clouds" cycle, you may notice that as the body becomes more relaxed through the release of stress and tension the visual color of the air exhaled begins to change from black to gray, perhaps even to off-white, a symbolic vision of complete relaxation.

Energy Breathing

Energy breathing is a way to vitalize your body, not only by taking in air through your nose or mouth but, in effect, by breathing through your whole body as well. In essence, your body acts like a big lung, taking in air and circulating it throughout your entire body.

There are three phases of this exercise, and you can do this technique either sitting or lying down. First, get comfortable and allow your shoulders to relax. If you choose to sit, try to keep your legs straight. Now, as you breathe in imagine that there is a circular hole at the top (crown) of your head, like a dolphin's spout. As air enters your lungs, visualize energy, in the form of a beam of light, entering the top of your head. Bring the energy down from the crown of your head to your abdomen as you inhale. As you exhale, allow the energy to leave through the top of your head. Repeat this five to ten times, trying to coordinate your breathing with the visual flow of energy. As you continue to bring the energy down to your stomach area, allow the light to reach all the inner parts of your upper body. When you feel comfortable with this first phase, you are ready to move on to the second phase.

Now, imagine that in the center of each foot there is a circular hole that energy can flow in and out of. Again, think of the energy as a beam of light. Concentrating on your lower extremities only, allow the flow of energy to move up from your feet into your abdomen as you inhale from your diaphragm. Repeat this five to ten times, trying to coordinate your breathing with the flow of energy.

Finally, as you continue to bring the energy up into your stomach area, allow the light to reach all the inner parts of your lower body. Once you feel you have established the coordination between your breathing and the visual flow of energy with your lower extremities, begin to combine the movement of energy down from the top of your head and up from your feet, bringing the energy to the center of your body as you inhale from your diaphragm. Then, as you exhale, allow the flow of energy to reverse the direction from which it came. Repeat this for ten to twenty times. Each time you move the energy through your body, feel each body region, each muscle and organ, and each cell become energized. At first it may seem difficult to visually coordinate the movement of energy coming from opposite ends of your body, but with practice this will become very easy.

One summer day while grocery shopping, I ran into a former student of mine, Tom, who is now a lieutenant in the Navy. Our conversation reminded me just how useful belly-breathing can be.

"You know, I used to think that all that breathing stuff you taught us in class was a crock," said Tom, a smile on his face. "But I don't anymore!"

Peering over a pyramid of apples, I inquired, "What changed your mind?"

"It was about a week before graduation, right, and I'm packing to move to Florida with my wife, to start flight school. Did I tell you she was eight months pregnant? OK, so I'm packing these boxes in the basement and Kathy tells me she's started going into labor. Not exactly good timing, know what I mean?"

Tom takes a step closer, grabbing an apple off the pyramid.

"Yup! You could say that my life was beyond the optimal stress point right about then. So here I am rushing to get Kathy to the hospital, but lo and behold, we get in the car only to find I have a flat tire. No problem, I tell her. Take a few deep breaths. I'll have this fixed in a jiffy.

"So now we're in the car headed to the hospital and guess what? Another flat tire, except this time I have no spare. I could go off to get help, but I can't leave my wife alone in the car. So you can only guess what happened.

"Man, that breathing stuff really worked. I kept telling her to take a deep breath, keep breathing, slow and deep, from the stomach, it will be all right. I was breathing right along with her. I'm not sure who it helped more, me or her. What an event! So now I'm the proud father of a little baby boy, Jonathan."

"Congratulations," I said, extending my hand.

"Thanks! You know, you always hear about babies being born in the backseat of a car, but I never thought mine would be one of them. And now, I'm doing that belly breathing technique every day."

> It is said that the soul enters the body with the first breath and each breath after invigorates the spirit. Remember to breathe—from the belly!

10

Animals With Souls

There are those who believe that the soul is a divine gift reserved only for humans, and that all other living things function at the level of basic instinct. The famous theologian Thomas Aquinas believed this. Of course, he also said that only men, not women, have souls. Every woman I know would take issue with this. Perhaps given the chance, animals would too.

Souls or not, there is something very calming about having a pet around. Current research reveals that pet owners typically have lower resting heart rates, lower resting blood pressure, quicker recovery time from illness, and, for the most part, are just basically healthier than non-pet owners. In looking for answers to explain the phenomena, researchers suggest that it is the pet owner's ability to express love which may be the significant factor in pet therapy. No hypothesis suggests that animals may themselves play an active role. That might presume that animals could think and even quite possibly have souls themselves. Perhaps they do!

It is a well-known fact that dogs seem to know when

their owners are about to come home. Perhaps you've seen a dog sit patiently by the door ready to greet its owner the moment he or she walks into the house. (By the way, it's thought that cats also are aware of their owners, but that they just don't care!) This fact sparked the attention and intrigue of several people, including British scientist Rupert Sheldrake.

Sheldrake designed a study to see if dogs really knew when their owners were coming home. The data apparently defies Western thought. With a split-timed video monitor, one camera on a dog at home with the owner's parents, the other on the owner an hour away, it was shown that the moment the owner made the conscious decision to return home and indeed started to do so, the dog got up off the floor and sat patiently by the door, awaiting the arrival of his owner. This was replicated several times with several different dogs and their owners. Equally interesting are the anecdotal stories of cats and dogs who have been known to travel hundreds (or thousands) of miles thorugh unfamiliar territory in France, Australia, Canada, and the United States to be reunited with their owners.

So how do pets know? Perhaps animals have a divine connection of which we are simply unaware, which manifests at times when we need to see it.

When it comes to animal heroics, there is no shortage of Good Samaritans. From dogs and cats to horses, canaries, and dolphins, the animal kingdom is rich in compassion. One of my favorite stories involves a little boy named George who stayed too late at the local public library one night, reading books on basketball. When he walked out the door to leave, it was dark. George knew his way home, and had traveled the route hundreds of times. On this night, though, as he passed the church on North 10th street, the hair raised on the back of his neck. He intuited danger. Sure enough, he was being followed.

George purposely crossed the street and tried to thwart the advances of the stranger, but he couldn't shake him off. Several blocks from the library, with less than a mile to go, George suddenly noticed a large dog walking at his heels, as if guarding him from danger. After a few more blocks, the man was nowhere to be seen. As George opened the gate to his yard, he reached his arm out to pet the dog on the head. Once inside, he begged his mother to come and look at his new companion. But having accomplished its mission, the dog had disappeared.

> Pets have a lot to offer (and perhaps teach) in terms of sharing joy, love, and relaxation. If you are looking for a reason to adopt a pet, keep this in mind.

11

Going for the Gold

In the doorway of my office stood a tall, daunting, muscular man about twenty years old. From the dimly lit desk, all I could see was a rather large silhouette. Not until he spoke did I recognize the voice. It was one of my advisees, Pedro, a transfer student from Spain.

"Do you have a minute?" he asked in quiet voice.

"Sure, come on in," I said, as I got up to greet him.

By nature, Pedro was a happy-go-lucky fellow. Perhaps due to his European background, he was more mature than most of his American contemporaries. Although his English was excellent, his Spanish accent was undeniable. With his ever-present smile, framed by a groomed beard, Pedro was a unique fixture on campus.

Closing the door to my office, Pedro instructed me to sit down. I could tell by his manner that he was very upset by something. "Can I trust you? I am about to tell you something which no one else knows. If you tell anyone, I will. . . ."

Shades of *The Princess Bride* came into my consciousness as I recalled one of the movie's most famous lines:

"My name is Inigo Montoya. You killed my father. Prepare to die!"

"You cannot tell anyone!" Pedro said.

"OK, Pedro. I promise," I replied in my most serious tone. "What is the problem?"

He pulled a sketch from his coat pocket and unfolded it. There lay a diagram of the Indian yogic chakras placed over an anatomical illustration of a male body. "Do you know what these are?" he inquired.

"Yes, they are chakras, the major energy centers of the body, part of the human energy field, " I said casually. This was a topic I had begun to introduce as a theory to my students regarding the not-yet-understood model of stress and disease. The word *chakra,* a Sanskrit word meaning "wheel," is not common to the American vernacular. I was impressed Pedro knew of this.

"Good!" Pedro said, slapping his hand on my desk. "Now we begin. I explain everything."

The story Pedro explained was like none I had ever heard before, certainly nothing that can be explained scientifically.

Pedro won the Olympic Bronze Medal in the 400-meter butterfly swimming event in Seoul, Korea, in 1988. The victory took several teams by surprise, including that of the Americans, but not Pedro. His determination was as strong as his movements in the water. Now, with an Olympic medal under his belt, he set his sights on the gold. As is common for international Olympic athletes, Pedro relocated to the United States to train with a new coach. Within a few months' time, he began having some serious health problems—heart palpitations, blood in the urine, muscle aches, and an overwhelming sense of fatigue. Pedro took every clinical test available. Each result came back negative. Doctors threw up their hands in defeat, not knowing what to make of his situation. Yet the symptoms continued for well over four months.

One day Pedro's mother called him from Madrid. It seems she had just come from the grocery store where she had overheard a conversation in the produce section. One of the two women speaking was the wife of Pedro's former swim coach. This woman confided to her friend that she had placed a spell on Pedro to make him ill, as punishment for abandoning the coach who had helped him win an Olympic medal. Pedro's mother gave him specific instructions: Find someone who understands these spiritual matters and have them help you. That afternoon, Pedro appeared at my door.

It was not uncommon to have people from all walks of life come to my office and inquire about matters of human spirituality and health, aspects of which Western science has yet to understand and quite often dismisses as nonsense. I had acquired a national reputation for creating a model of human spirituality with regard to relationships, values, and a meaningful purpose in life. Not all of human spirituality, however, was so neatly packaged. On campus, I also had the reputation of, if nothing more, at least being willing to listen to people tell of everything from near-death experiences and past-life regressions to alien abduction. This, however, was the first time I had ever heard about witchcraft, a practice I was to learn was not uncommon in Spain. While Pedro's condition was not fatal, there was no telling how serious the events could turn. So far, the spell had done its work. At the rate of deterioration, Pedro would never make it to the next Olympics, let alone win a Gold Medal.

With the look of a lost, destitute tourist, Pedro said, "So, can you help me?"

"To be quite honest," I said, "this is out of my league." (Boy, was *that* an understatement!) Before I could continue, Pedro lowered his head in despair. "But, I know someone who can."

"Really? Who?" Pedro said, bouncing back to life.

As it turned out, I had just finished taking a yearlong course in bio-energy medicine with a world-famous healer named Mietek Wirkus in Bethesda, Maryland. A Polish emigrant to the United States, Mietek has the ability to see chakras, auras, and disease states in the human energy field. Better than a CAT scan, his accuracy rate is about 95 percent. Using a technique he calls bio-energy, Mietek works to clear distortions in the energy field, bringing the body back to a sense of balance and wholeness. In one aspect, bio-energy would be no different than Western medicine if there wasn't the responsibility on the part of the client to do some internal work, too. For the client, meditation, visualization, and prayer constitute the dynamics of bio-energy as well.

At first Pedro's situation seemed unique, if not bizarre. But as I mulled it over, I realized that at some level it was no different than any other mind-body-spirit health issue. We all encounter some aspect of darkness or fear, whether our own or others'. Perhaps distilled fear is best labeled as "evil." Regardless of its source, it is fear which we must learn to overcome—with love. Sometimes we can do it ourselves, sometimes we need help. Always with God's grace.

I called Mietek's office, talked to his secretary, and

made an appointment. Mietek took Pedro right away. Mietek never mentioned an evil spell. In his terminology, there are only "disturbances" and "congestions" in the human energy field. This is what he worked on with Pedro. After two sessions of bio-energy, Pedro's symptoms disappeared, never to return again. Within weeks he was back to his arduous training routine.

"Let me teach you some Spanish," Pedro said one afternoon outside my office. "I'm gonna teach you how to say 'gold medal.' Repeat after me: *'medalla de'oro.'*"

> Fear, even in its worst form—evil—can be dealt with and reconciled over time. We must take the first step toward decreasing the toxic effects of distilled fear. And there is strength in numbers, for there are always those who can help us.

section five

Working the Funny Bone

HAVE YOU EVER FOUND YOURSELF SAYING, right after hell breaks loose, "A year from now, this *might* be funny, but right now, it's not funny!" I say, why wait a whole year to laugh?

Spiritual muscles attach to spiritual bones and, let there be no doubt—the funny bone is a crucial one! Ask anyone who has undergone a personal crisis, and most likely they will tell you how at some point a ray of humor, from a quantum sliver to a Disney rainbow, appeared.

Perhaps it's no surprise to learn that many Nazi concentration camp survivors and Vietnam POWs have cited humor as a critical component of their path to freedom. We would be wise to follow their lead regardless of our situation, whether it's a flat tire, an endless game of phone-tag, locking your keys in your car, or having your child accidentally flush your wallet down the toilet. How about traffic jams? We could all use a good laugh then. The following stories are reminders of what we already know, that humor is essential to deal with stress.

Freud called humor a defense mechanism for the ego. Others refer to comic relief as "the grand coping technique." Regardless of what you call it, you get more bang for your buck when you crack a smile in the face of adversity. And besides, just think, at the very end, how many new pearly gate jokes St. Peter will tell you before you walk in to collect your wings.

"So there were these two poets at the gates of heaven and St. Peter says, 'Hi guys. Sorry, but right now, we only have one vacancy. The one with the best poem gets in. . . . And you have to use the word *Timbuktu.*' "

1

Laughter *Is* the Best Medicine

To see the twinkle in her eyes and the genuine smile that graces her face, you would never know that Donna was a recovering cocaine addict or that the addiction had nearly killed her. The twinkle and smile reveal what the mask of cocaine had hidden for years. I met her when we were both faculty members of the University of Colorado's Center for Human Caring. At lunch one day we discussed how humor had been our saving grace in times of trouble.

Humor comes to us from the same root as the words *fluid* or *moisture*. "Humor is about having a fluid spirit," explains Donna, and she would know, because humor therapy has become her calling. Right up front, Donna will tell you she is an overachiever. By age nineteen, she had earned a Bachelor's degree in nursing. By twenty, she received her Master's. Perhaps it was an attempt to please her parents, perhaps it was an attempt to fill a void, but whatever Donna did, she excelled at—exceptionally well. But the road to success was not without its potholes. During her junior year in college, she began to use speed, which then led to alcohol, which in turn led to cocaine—a downward spiral toward the edge of death.

"Back when I was in school, you could get a doctor's prescription for amphetamines. A lot of people took them to lose weight. I took them so I could stay up late and study." As Donna describes it, where there is speed to bring you up, there is alcohol to bring you down, and she soon found herself becoming dependent on both substances to achieve a false sense of balance in her life. By twenty-three, Donna was married and her professional career in nursing was skyrocketing. However, alcohol had become a constant friend and it was soon joined by cocaine as her drug of choice for what she calls the last three years of her eleven-year addiction history.

"Where did I get the cocaine?" she asks with a giggle. "I got it from several of the physicians with whom I worked. You know, one out of every five cocaine addicts is a white-collar professional. We're not all street bums. The first time I used cocaine, I loved it. But what it was doing was filling a void. Cocaine was a magic bullet. It took me away from my childhood pain. It also ruined my life. I knew eventually I was going to die."

Ironically, even though Donna worked as a psychiatric nurse with the chronically mental ill, her colleagues never suspected she had an addiction problem. "As a rule, health care professionals who are addicts tend to be overachievers. Even on a bad day, we still look pretty good. It never occurred to anyone that I had a drug problem. Everyone loved me and cared for me. My friends and colleagues were enablers. They thought I was depressed because I was going through a divorce, so they helped me by covering for me and doing some of my work. It kept me sick longer."

Donna put up a good front but eventually the habit began to take its toll. She spent over a quarter of a million dollars servicing her addiction in a three-year period. She looked run-down and depressed (she lost thirty pounds, and was down to ninety pounds), and the quality of her work performance suffered dramatically. As the signs and symptoms of an addiction became more evident, a friend began to see through the lies and deceptions and one day called her on the carpet.

Sensing she was suicidal and ready to die, her friend called Donna's parents in a successful attempt to get her some help. Almost by force, Donna quit her job and entered a thirty-day treatment program. It was the beginning of a very long road to recovery. From the month long treatment program, she entered a halfway house for three months (a humbling experience, she admits) and then continued as an outpatient for the next nine months, all the while undergoing psychoanalysis treatment and attending Alcoholics Anonymous and Cocaine Anonymous meetings, which, years later, she still attends regularly.

"It was my sister who taught me the importance of silliness. It was my grandmother who gave me strength, hope, and inspiration." This special alchemy turned to gold in the course of her recovery. "This may sound silly," she said, "but in treatment, we did meditation and visualization. Three times a wizard came to me with a message either on a scroll or in a crystal ball. The message was one word—humor. It was then I knew I needed to pursue the issue of laughter as a means to cope. I needed to learn to lighten up. So I studied with Annette Goodheart, Steve Allen Jr., and Bernie Siegel."

With her natural talent for public speaking, Donna's future was cast in mirth. Today she is considered an expert in the field of humor therapy, traveling extensively throughout the international community to share the benefits of humor and laughter.

The twinkle in her eyes, the smile on her face and the laugh in her voice say it all.

> God gave us humor so we could laugh at ourselves, and not take ourselves too seriously.

2

You Know You're Having a Bad Day When...

Sometimes making light of a bad situation helps take the edge off. That's what humor therapy is all about. When we can separate ourselves from our problems, we gain a much better perspective on them. Humor can help us get to that broader perspective more quickly. One of the elements of humor is the art of exaggeration, a technique used by nearly every stand-up comic: "My mother-in-law is so frugal, if you look up the word cheapskate in the dictionary, you'll see her picture there."

It seems that by taking things to the extreme, we gain a proper perspective on the truth, especially those embarrassing moments where humor may be the only relief. In several of my workshops, I invite participants to exaggerate what a worst possible day could look like by filling in the blank. It doesn't take long for them to realize that by doing so, their day doesn't look so bad after all. Here are some of their responses:

You know you're having a bad day when . . .

1. More than two cops pull you over for a speeding ticket.
2. Strange lights start flashing on your dashboard, and you know you're not driving Chitty Chitty Bang Bang!
3. You get called into the boss' office and within moments, there are two security guards at the door to escort you.
4. You get a letter from the IRS inviting you to an audit—yours!
5. Your girlfriend says she's pregnant and you've had a vasectomy.
6. The bank calls to tell you they mistakenly credited your checking account with $2,500 a few months ago, and they want their money back.
7. You sit down to enjoy a night of television and when you start surfing you see your name and photograph on America's Most Wanted.
8. Your boss catches you after hours sitting on the photocopy machine—butt-naked, about to hit the start button.
9. Your son calls, asking for money to go to college, and to the best of your knowledge, you don't have any children.
10. You get up early, shower, fix breakfast, and head to work, only to find out it's Saturday.

11. You go in for your yearly physical exam and your doctor asks if you'd like to be an organ donor.
12. The car you got for graduation turns out to be a lemon rather than a pumpkin.
13. Your wife comes home from work and tells you she's in love, but as she goes into detail, you quickly realize it's not with you.

> You know you're having a good day when you can't think of a bad day to compare it to.

3

Test Anxiety

Picture this. You're a college student sitting in a classroom taking a midterm or final exam. This is not your only exam this week. Perhaps you even already had two this very same day. You're tired and the information you crammed into your brain last night is leaking out uncontrollably with each breath. All you want to do is finish this exam, go home, and sleep.

The professor passes out the test. Tension hangs heavy in the air. You glance at each page. Anxiety sets in as you realize there are things you just don't know. You didn't study this stuff! You go back to the first page and start with what you do know. Part I: Multiple choice, then multiple guess. Done! Now on to Part II: Definition of Terms. Again you do the ones you know first. Then you backtrack and stare at the others on which you remain clueless. An idea strikes you. Put something down—anything. If you don't know the real answer, make one up. If you *really* don't know, be even more creative. Maybe you'll get points for imagination. Who knows? Give it a try. Don't forget the final essay!

Now picture this. You're a college professor who has just given a midterm or final exam. You drive home with a stack of forty, sixty, perhaps even eighty exams to grade. The initial thought does not excite you. This will wait till the weekend, you think. The weekend comes and you pull out a red pen and start with Part I: Multiple Choice. That was easy. Just match the letters (a, b, c, d) with the key. Now comes Part II: Definition of Terms. On the third exam, you break out laughing. You laugh even harder on the fifth exam. Entirely wrong but creative answers are your salvation for the next few hours.

Einstein once said that imagination is more powerful than knowledge. He must have thought this after grading some college exams. The following are some answers to exam questions by students in moments of creativity, imagination, and desperation which I have collected over the years. The laughter they have engendered has been my saving grace during the long midnight hours of grading exams.

Nutrition, Health, and Performance Exam:

Define the following terms with one or two sentences and give an example where appropriate.

1. Free Radical

   Real answer: An aberrant oxygen molecule associated with disease and the aging processes. Example: transfatty acids.

   Student's answer: A liberated politician, example: Nelson Mandela (ha ha!)

2. BMR

Real answer: Basal Metabolic Rate, the number of calories one burns at complete rest in a twenty-four hour period, approximately 2000 calories.

Student's answer: Bowel Movement Reaction? Boy, could I use one right now to relieve some stress. (I wasn't here that night in class.)

3. Circle of Poison

Real answer: Illegal pesticides manufactured in the U.S. are sold to other countries which use them on various acricultural products which are then sold back to U.S. markets.

Student's answer: The food my wife serves me every night for dinner.

Student's answer: The food court at the local mall!

4. Peristalsis

Real answer: A wave-like muscular contraction moving food from the mouth to the rectum.

Student's answer: I think this is a fatal disease from eating too much junk food.

5. Echinacea

Real answer: An herb used to boost the immune system for colds and flu.

Student's answer: A deadly bacteria second only to the e-boli virus. This should be avoided at all costs!

6. Healthy Food Guidelines

    Real answer: A list of suggestions to improve eating behaviors. Example: Decrease consumption of saturated fats such as cheese and butter.

    Student's answer: Don't eat the yellow snow?

7. Aspartame

    Real answer: Artificial sugar substitute found in Nutrasweet.

    Student's answer: wild guess—the guy who discovered broccoli?

8. Homogenization

    Real answer: The process by which fat molecules are equally distributed in milk.

    Student's answer: This is when two lesbians or a gay couple decide to have a baby. Example: My sister and her lover adopted a little boy.

9. Candida

    Real answer: A yeast infection in the gastrointestinal track which can lead to cravings for sweets and weight gain.

    Student answer: The country north of the United States. (Wink!)

Stress Management Exam

Define the following terms with one or two sentences and give an example where appropriate.

1. Entrainment Theory

    Real answer: The mutual phase-locking of like vibrations. Example: music therapy for relaxation.

    Student's answer: This is a typo. It should be Entertainment Theory. Entertainment Theory describes being entertained to relax. Example: the movie *Scream*.

2. Hardy Personality

    Real answer: A composite of personality traits to make one hardy against the pressures of stress.

    Student's answer: A fictional personality to overcome stress. Example: The Hardy Boys.

3. Koan

    Real Answer: An unsolvable puzzle used in meditation to reach enlightenment. Example: What is the sound of one hand clapping?

    Student's answer: The Ark of the Lost Covenant. Example: "Indiana Jones."

4. Glucocorticoids

    Real answer: Hormones secreted by the adrenal gland during the fight-or-flight response.

    Student's answer: A nutritious food supplement for a well-balanced diet—high in sugar, low in fat. Example: Twinkie—I eat these all the time (smile!)

5. Synestasia

   Real answer: An experience in meditation where sensory crossover occurs. Example, one can see sounds and hear colors.

   Student's answer: Isn't Synestasia the hit sequel to the Disney movie, *Anastasia*?

> Perhaps Einstein was right—imagination is more powerful than knowledge. It's definitely more amusing.

4

Grace

I am frequently a dinner guest at my good friend Holly's home. She has two adolescent boys, Steven and Shane. Steven is a rebel without a cause; Shane is the embodiment of joy and wonder. They complement each other quite nicely. Since her divorce, Holly has tried to introduce several new rituals to her boys. The one I observed and on several occasions have participated in is the ritual said before the evening meal—grace.

A spiritual (not religious) person, Holly purchased the books *Earth Prayers* and *The Little Zen Book* as the catalyst for this ritual. The tradition begins with selecting a poem from either book. Each person takes a turn. Typically, the boys, ages ten and twelve, fight not to go first, but last, and this too has become part of the ritual.

One night after each of us had read a poem, I asked if we could join hands. Reluctantly, each boy gave Holly and myself a pinkie and I quickly said, "Amen."

Without missing a beat, Steven said, "What does *amen* mean?"

I replied, "It's a way of saying thanks," hoping not to instigate a fight, but it was too late.

"Who are we saying thanks to?" he asked with angst. "We're not saying thanks to God, because there is no God." With a voice of complete defiance and fork in hand, he yelled, "I don't believe in God!"

Not wishing to start an argument, I refrained from delving into the topic. But it was too late. Steven was just getting started.

"There is no God," he said. With a brazen look that would have stopped the Crusades, he continued, "There is a name for this, you know." Looking me dead in the eye, he stated, "My friends call me . . ." then he paused. "My friends call me . . ." and he paused again. Then breaking character, his eyes rolled left up to the ceiling, searching for the word he so desperately wanted.

After a moment, he regained his composure, fixed a stare in my direction, and said with the utmost confidence,

"My friends call me an *amethyst.*"

> Art Linkletter, quoting a passage from Proverbs, often said, "Out of the mouths of babes, oft times come gems." Children may be the source of stress at times, but they are also a mine for precious gems. Keep an eye and ear open for these gems each and every day.

5

Jesus With a Smile

There are many theories which try to explain the reasons why we laugh and giggle, ranging from Plato's superiority theory (laughing at others to make ourselves feel good, for instance Dan Quayle jokes), to Freud's release/relief theory (laughter as a sexual release, such as Bill Clinton jokes). Then there are those who insist that humor is simply a gift from God, hence the name the Divinity Theory.

Human spirituality is based on relationships, and humor certainly creates a bond between those who laugh together. Humor, it is said, is the shortest distance between two people. The Divinity Theory is alive and well when you consider the humorous nature of the Dalai Lama, who promotes laughter as a means to cleanse the spirit. A study into indigenous cultures reveals that the role of a healer bears traits similar to those of the American circus clown. Does God have sense of humor? Most theologians think (and hope) so.

I first came across this idea in a book by Cal Samra, *The Joyful Christ: The Healing Power of Humor.* Inside, I found something I had never before seen—illustrations of Jesus actually smiling. To be honest, most depictions looked more like my college roommates, but nonetheless, I was amused.

Samra and others like him highlight specific references to the mirth and merriment in the New Testament (somehow I must have missed this in church). Whereas it is written that Jesus wept, to my knowledge there is no direct passage citing Jesus having a good belly-laugh. However, reading between the lines you can find inferences and suppositions leading you to believe such an event must have occurred sometime in his life. If not in his first thirty-three years, perhaps sometime after. . . .

One person who shares this perspective is Gladys Taylor McGary, M.D., affectionately known as the grandmother of alternative medicine. Raised in India by two American physicians, Gladys was destined to become a physician herself. Perhaps it was part Eastern mysticism, but Gladys knew there was more to healing than the standard Western medical approach of drugs and surgery. Concerned by what she saw as uncompassionate health care, she helped form the American Holistic Medical Association in 1978. This organization was founded on the belief that to be healthy, *all* aspects—mind, body, spirit, and emotions—must be considered in the treatment of each individual.

Gladys will tell you that humor is one of the most important healing agents for optimal well-being, even in the face of death. This story is one she shared with me over dinner one evening at the National Wellness Conference in Steven's Point, Wisconsin.

"I often tell my patients not to fear death. Death is a transitional stage. It is nothing to be afraid of, I say. One day during my rounds, one of my patients related this experience," Gladys said with a gleam in her eye. He said:

"I was lying on my bed, just waiting to die. I prayed and prayed for God to take me. Just then I saw a vision: It was an apparition of Jesus on the cross, as big as life—right in front of me. He opened his eyes and looked at me. I could tell he was suffering. I was suffering too. I looked at Jesus and said, 'Can you help me?'

The next thing I knew, I saw Jesus reach his hand down to me. I was surprised because his hands are supposed to be nailed to the cross. So I said, 'Jesus, how can you reach your hand to me when you're nailed to the cross. How do you stay up there?'

And with a smile, Jesus said to me, 'Velcro.' "

If Jesus can smile at his plight, so can we at our own!

6

Laughing at Myself

It has been said that most of us take ourselves too seriously, especially at work. Generally speaking, we take ourselves far too seriously in every aspect of life. An ancient proverb says that God gave us humor so that we could laugh at ourselves. I come across a great many people, however, who seem to have cashed in this divine gift for a perpetual frown. While it may be easy to laugh at other people's misfortunes, we are not so likely to do the same with our own. As a rule, we don't share "most embarrassing" stories until the ego's bruises are well healed, various people involved are deceased, or we can embellish the details for added effect.

My sense of humor has definitely grown over the years. It was my college roommate at the University of Maine who first gave my funnybone a workout. A kid at heart, Tom typically would fill his quota of more than 500 laughs a day. Gladly, I followed his lead. Today, my humor muscle is seven times its original size. Now, like everyone, I have had my share of embarrassing moments, some which I am sure I have repressed deep in my unconscious, but here is one that I gladly repeat:

Three months into my first book tour, I stopped in Columbus, Ohio, to visit Tom, my former college roommate. To no one's surprise, he was still filling his humor quota daily—even with two infants. The second day of my visit, Tom drove me to a local bookstore, where I was to do a presentation and book signing. Moments after I walked in the front door, I pulled out my fountain pen, which I used for autographing books, only to have it bleed all over my hands. Feeling foolish (you don't get a second chance to make a first impression), I quickly ran to the bathroom to wash my hands, but it was too late. The ink had dried and nothing I did removed the mess.

While in the bathroom, I decided to make use of the facilities, but when I looked around I only saw stalls, no urinals. The first thought that hit me was that this was one of those new bathrooms. Then it dawned on me. In my haste, I had run into the women's rest room. Just as I realized my mistake, a woman entered, looked at me in horror, and let out a scream.

I could have panicked, I suppose, but in my moment of embarrassment, I opted for humor. In the thickest fake-European accent I could muster, I muttered, "I no speaka anglish," and quickly ran out the door.

A half-hour later I began my discussion as people filed in and took a seat in the back of the store. At one point, I looked up to see the same lady I had encountered in the women's bathroom. I waved my ink-stained hand and she smiled at me for the entire duration of my talk. Inside I was smiling too!

The ego reacts, the soul responds. Allow yourself permission to respond rather than react so that you may be guided by spirit always.

7

A Good Day in Hell

Life is full of tests, but in college the tests are of a different nature: the grade shows up on your report card, etched in stone for life. There is always that one student who, after getting a bad grade, will beat your door down to get some extra credit in the hope of resurrecting his or her GPA. The offers range from writing a twenty-page term paper to washing your car for a whole semester—anything to expunge the failed grade.

One of my colleagues, Robert Schambaugh, Ph.D., at the University of Oklahoma's Department of Engineering, is well-known for including an open-ended essay question on his exams to see just how well his students can synthesize information, rather than simply regurgitating it back. He has been known to ask such questions as "Why do airplanes fly?" One day during a phone conversation, our talk turned to the occasional student who sits and stares at the exam, unable to write much of anything. Stunned, the student walks out of the classroom, seeking a hint of insight and some academic mercy. Perhaps walking across the campus quad, the idea strikes: Hey! Maybe there is way to reverse the failed grade!

Was it extra credit that prompted one student to reorganize his thoughts and give another go at one of Dr. Schambaugh's "alleged" essay questions, perhaps even with a wider audience? What better way to vindicate oneself from the embarrassment of academic humiliation. Dr. Schambaugh could only guess at the motive.

Now this may be a case of *extra* extra credit, or it may be some goodhearted fun, but an answer to this now-infamous essay test question has recently circulated well beyond the halls of academia out onto the Internet.

"I have gotten phone calls and e-mails from all over the world on this. I'm sorry to say that it never happened. Yes, it's true I ask open-ended questions, but this is not the kind of question I would ask." Then, with a pause, he added, "Perhaps it's a former student trying to make amends. I don't know."

Did the Professor think the effort was totally in vain? "No, it is clever and pretty funny," he added, laughing on the phone.

Extra Credit Essay Question

"Is hell exothermic or endothermic? Support your answer with proof."

"First, we postulate that if souls exist, they must have some mass. If they do, then a mole of souls also must have a mass. So, at what rate are souls moving into hell and at what rate are souls leaving? I think we can safely assume that once a soul gets to hell, it does not leave.

"Therefore, no souls are leaving. As for souls entering hell, let's look at the different religions that exist in the world today. Some religions say that if you are not a member of their religion, you will go to hell. Since there is more than one of these religions, and people do not belong to more than one religion, we can project that all people and all souls go to hell. With the birth and death rates what they are, we can expect the number of souls in hell to increase exponentially.

"Now, we look at the rate of change in the volume of hell. Boyle's Law states that in order for the temperature and pressure in hell to stay the same, the ratio of the mass of the souls and volume needs to stay constant.

"[A1] If hell is expanding at a slower rate than the rate at which souls enter hell, then the temperature and pressure in hell will increase until all Hell breaks loose.

"[A2] However, if hell is expanding at a rate faster than the increase in souls in hell, then the temperature and pressure will drop until hell freezes over.

"So which is it? If we accept the postulate given to me by Theresa Banyan during my freshman year, that 'It'll be a cold day in hell before I sleep with you,' and taking into account that I still have not succeeded in having sexual relations with her, then [A2] cannot be true. Thus, hell is exothermic."

A good day in hell beats a bad day in hell anytime. Go for the extra credit!

8

Making Andrew Laugh

As part of an effort to expand the curriculum in our department of Health and Fitness at American University in fall 1990, I was asked if I would create a new elective. I knew immediately what course I wanted to teach. A firm believer in the positive power of humor, I decided to create a spinoff from one of my stress management lectures on humor therapy and create a course on "Humor and Health." At first I was laughed at by fellow faculty members and upper-level administrators, but within weeks the course was approved.

No sooner did the course appear on the registration catalog than the enrollment filled up. For the next several weeks my phone rang off the hook with students offering me their firstborn to get into the class. Their efforts were in vain. It was explained to me that due to space limitations, there was a limit of thirty students (and thirty chairs). No exceptions! A lot of students hung up disgruntled. This part was not funny.

One day the phone rang and a voice on the other end said, "Hi, this is Andrew. I'm calling because I want to enroll in your humor class and it's booked up. Is there any way I can get in?"

I replied, "I'm sorry Andrew, I can't help you. There is only room for thirty people and thirty chairs. My hands are tied. There is no more room."

"Fine," said Andrew, "I'll be right over." And with that, I heard a click and a dial tone.

About ten minutes later, I heard an electronic buzz outside my office door, and wondered what it was. Seconds later a wheelchair came cruising into my office. The man in the chair held up both arms and said, "Hi, I'm Andrew."

Impressed by his persistence, but adamant about the situation, I said, "Andrew, I'm sorry, but things haven't changed in the last ten minutes. There is still no room in the class."

He said, "Do you have time to hear my story?" Without waiting for a reply, he began.

"The day after I turned thirteen, the day before school was to start, I was swimming with my brother in the backyard pool. It's not like you think. I didn't hit my head in the shallow end. To this day the doctors can't explain it. All I know is that the angle in which I entered the water in the deep end was wrong. My neck snapped and, at age thirteen, I became a quadriplegic. I was in the hospital rehab wing for almost a year.

"Every day after lunch, a nurse would come in and say to me, 'Do you want to hear the joke of the day?' If I could have used my arms, I would have pulled the sheets up over me, but all I could do was turn my head away. I thought she would give up and go away, but no, she proceeded to tell me the joke. This went on for several months.

"One day she came into the room and I, of course,

turned my head. But this time I must have had my guard down, because when she told the joke, I laughed. I laughed for about twenty minutes. I think I laughed for all the times I wanted to laugh, but didn't.

"And you know what?" Andrew asked. "On that day I realized that I was on the road to recovery." As he said this he raised his arms up off the chair bars. "Now I am not going to say that humor has cured me, but it sure has helped in the recovery process.

"I'm a first-semester senior and life is extremely tough. I'm applying to medical school, but I am having a tough time getting in. My funny bone has atrophied considerably. Is there any possible way I can get into your humor class? I really need it."

By now, my eyes looked like a miniature version of Niagara Falls. Wiping a tear, I said, "Andrew, for you I'll make an exception."

And with that he said, "Good! And I even have my own chair!"

As it turns out, Andrew was a much better teacher than student in that course. On the last day of the semester, Andrew drove his wheelchair up to me and said, "I want you to make me a promise."

"OK," I replied, "What is it?"

"Raise your hand," he said.

I raised my right hand as if I was in a court of law and waited to take an oath.

"Promise me that whenever you teach people about humor, you will try to make them laugh. People take themselves way too seriously. We all need to laugh more. Look at me, if I can do it, anybody can. There is no excuse."

"Andrew," I said, "I promise!"

So to honor my pledge to Andrew, I share with you this joke that I heard told by Garrison Keillor on his radio show *Prairie Home Companion.* And yes, it did make Andrew laugh.

Three couples signed up at a local church for a premarriage counseling workshop. As they sat down in the church auditorium, the pastor greeted them and then started with these words, "Before we continue any further I must tell you that to be a member of this church in good standing, there must be no sexual relations prior to the marriage ceremony. Is that understood?" All three couples nodded their heads in agreement, and the minister proceeded with the content of his workshop. Before he dismissed the group, he again reminded each couple of their promise of chastity, and told them he would see them again in two weeks.

Two weeks later, the three couples were seated in front of the minister, ready to continue the second of the two-part workshop.

"Before I begin, I must ask you in good faith: did everyone abide by my rule?" he asked.

The first couple, both in their sixties, raised their hands. Then the elderly man spoke, "Well pastor, it really wasn't a problem. Although we are living together, we simply slept in separate bedrooms for the past two weeks. We barely even kissed."

"Good!" said the minister, "Now what about you?" directing his question to the second couple, in their forties.

"Well," the woman replied, "it wasn't easy. Like the first couple we are living together. We ended up sleeping in separate beds. It was a stretch for two weeks, but we did it."

"Good!" said the minister. Then turning to the youngest couple, he inquired, "Now how about you two folks?"

There was a long pause. Then the twenty-two-year-old man responded. "Well sir, we were doing rather well the first week. We didn't even hold hands. Then one day I saw my fiancée reach up on a shelf for a light bulb, and to be honest, I got rather excited. All of a sudden she dropped the package and bent down to pick it up. I couldn't help myself, sir. For the next half-hour we made passionate love on the floor." As he said this, he looked down to the ground.

The minister looked extremely disappointed. Holding his anger, he stood up and said, "I am sorry, but you are not allowed in this church."

And the young man answered, "You think that's bad, we're not allowed in the grocery store either."

Let a smile be your umbrella—and follow Andrew's advice to lighten up!

9

American Graffiti

Research shows that a child typically laughs between 300 to 400 times a day. But by the time we reach adulthood the number drops below fifteen. Hospital patients, it is noted, never reach the threshold of one laugh per day. While humor may be the best medicine, comic relief is in critically short supply in our health care system.

Rather than assign a term paper to the students taking my Humor and Health class, I decided to be more creative and have them do a more functional, meaningful project. In trying to instill some lifelong health behaviors, I created an assignment called the Tickler Notebook. The premise of this project was to have the students compile a collection of jokes, comics, cards, photographs, and stories—anything that would put a smile on their face.

"You never know," I said. "One day you might just find yourself in need of this, if you ever end up in the hospital. So have it ready to pack up with your toothbrush and PJs." The project met with tremendous success. Ten years later, I still get cards and letters from students telling me they are on their fifth or sixth notebook.

Metaphorically speaking, humor is a two-way street. Humor may be a perception we take in but it is also something we can share. Such was the case, I was to learn, with the Tickler Notebook.

Christine Flanagan, R.N., an oncology nurse at Shady Grove Adventist Hospital in Rockville, Maryland, was a guest speaker in my class one night. She told the class how she had applied and received a grant to create a humor cart for the oncology ward that she supervised. The cart, a red wagon, was filled with videos, audiocassettes, cartoon books, and various other items that could be used to lift the spirits of the cancer patients. Her intention was to integrate humor into the healing process and do something about the dearth of laughter at work.

The students were mesmerized by her story. Inspiration struck them like a bolt of lightening. Like a modern version of the classic fable "Stone Soup," students began to offer Christine items from their Tickler Notebooks as a donation to the humor cart.

Aside from the many humorous items collected, a drive was organized in class by one student to find the funniest graffiti and compile a list to include in the Tickler Notebook compendium. Here are a few excerpts to tickle your funnybone (and possibly add to your own Tickler Notebook):

On Education

- Lately, there has been an alarming increase in things about which I know absolutely nothing.
- You can be a business major and be cool, but there aren't too many of us.

- I thought drugs were fun, till I started studying pharmacology.
- Linguistics is the exact opposite of screaming.
- Graffiti may be funny, but it won't get you tenure.
- God created the world in seven days, but it took him four years to graduate from this place.
- God didn't create the world in seven days, he partied for six and pulled an all-nighter.
- Riddle me this, all you existential Med Students:

  How many amino acids can dance on the head of a pin?

  A: It depends on the music.

  A: Would it be acid rock?

  A: How about "pro-teen angel?"
- Please Remember! Today's lesson: Bullwinkle is...

  A: How a cow knows for sure.
- If you took all the students that sleep in class and laid them down end to end, they'd be a lot more comfortable.

On Politics

- The trouble with America is that so many jokes get elected!
- If "pro" is the opposite of "con," what is the opposite of progress?
- The difference between capitalism and communism is that in capitalism, man exploits man. Under communism, it's the other way around.

On Philosophy

Old Plato saw both mind and matter,
Thomas Hobbes saw but the latter.
Now Thom's soul doth rot in hell;
Quoth God, "It's immaterial."

Q: Why is there air?

A: Have you ever tried breathing Cool Whip?

- Adam was God's rough draft!

Q: Did you know that ignorance and apathy are the two biggest problems on college campus?

A: I don't know and I don't care

- God is love,
  Love is blind,
  Ray Charles is blind,
  Therefore . . .

On Life

- It's better to be rich and happy than poor and unhappy.

  Are the poor so unhappy? Are the rich so happy?

  I've been rich and I've been poor. Believe me, the rich are happier.

- No man is an island, but when you piss urination (you're a nation).
- I complained because I had no shoes until I met a man who had no credit cards.

- Abstain from wine, women, and song—mostly song.
- All I ask for is the chance to prove that money cannot buy happiness.
- Why is it that when you talk to God, it's called praying, but when God talks to you, it's called schizophrenia?
- World's shortest lists:
    1. Creative accountants.
    2. Honest politicians.
    3. Good American cars.
    4. Graffitiests who kan spell rite.
    5. Consecutive winning seasons at Iowa.

On Sex

- Panties may not be the best thing in the world, but they're next to it!
- Grapenuts is not a venereal disease!
- If I told you you had a beautiful body, would you hold it against me?
- Contraceptives should be used at every conceivable moment.
- It's hard to find a good man, but oh, it's good to find a hard man.
- The sexual life of a male: tri-weekly; try weekly; try weakly.

There once was a gaucho named Bruno
Who said sex is one thing I do know!
Sheep are just fine

Women divine
But llama are numero uno!

In the Garden of Eden lay Adam
Complacently stroking his madam
And great was his mirth
For he knew that on earth
There were only two balls, and he had 'em!

A timorous Viking named Kord
Got seasick when aboard
Until Princess Vale
Enticed him to sail
His longboat the length of her fjörd!

There once was a monk from Algeria
Whose knowledge was somewhat inferior
One night of fun
With a comely young nun
And now she's mother superior

Imponderables

- If a sheep is a ram, and a donkey is an ass, how come a ram in the ass is a goose?
- How come there's no ham in hamburger?
- Why do we drive on a parkway and park on a driveway?
- If Jesus was a Jew, how come he has a Puerto Rican name?
- Why is Octoberfest always held in September?
- Can a blue man sing the whites?

- Is Dogma the mother of all dogs?
- If corn oil comes from corn, and coconut oil comes from coconuts, where does baby oil come from?

Odds and Ends

- Graffiti: the poetry of the simpleminded.
- Human: An erudite ape with less hair and more money.
- College student: A pre-erudite ape with more hair and less money.
- You exist, it's this place that is unreal.
- There is no gravity, the earth sucks!
- I've been all over this universe, and take my word for it, Earth makes the best popcorn!
- For those of you who think that life is a joke, consider the punchline.
- I was here, where were you? Be back soon.

  —Godot
- You only go around once, but if you work it out right, once is enough!

> Humor (Vitamin H) is an essential nutrient for mental, spiritual, emotional, and physical well-being. Be sure to take your supplement today and get your RDA of laughter.

section six

Silver Linings and Lemonade

IT HAS BEEN SAID THAT THE SUBTLE DIFFERENCE between an optimist and a pessimist is just three letters. In truth, the difference is one of perception. Driving down the street one day, I saw a bumper sticker: "One's attitude is the real disability." It turned out that the driver was physically impaired (but not disabled); she had Multiple Sclerosis. At the grocery store, she parked her car and limped, ever so gracefully, toward the entrance.

When I first ran the Boston Marathon, on a cold, wet

day in 1978, like many other runners around me, I began to moan in anticipation of Heartbreak Hill, a seven-mile incline toward the end of the race. Just as I was about to turn to my college roommate and complain about a cramp in my left leg, I was passed by an athlete in a wheelchair who had no legs. Four more wheelchair athletes followed him, in pursuit. At that same moment, the sun broke through the clouds. The symbology was powerful. Attitude is everything! It turns lemons into lemonade, and at the end of any race, this is truly the thirst quencher.

One component of optimism is healthy self-esteem—believing the good about you. So, in addition to stories about simple pleasures and healthy attitudes, this section highlights self-esteem through four components: mentors and role models, uniqueness, empowerment, and connectedness. Perhaps as you read these chapters you might consider how you can begin to augment your self-esteem so that life's problems will be inclined to roll off your back. And when you cross the finish line of your particular challenge, you too can enjoy the lemonade and sunshine.

1

Positive Affirmations

One should never underestimate the power of high self-esteem when dealing with stress. When your self-esteem is high, then everyday problems, both big and small, roll right off your back. However, when self-esteem is low, it's as if you become a bull's-eye target, begging to be hit.

Self-esteem is hard to keep high when we badmouth ourselves. Like an obnoxious talk radio host, the ego babbles incessantly, constantly giving us subliminal negative feedback that we are never "good enough." One of the first methods of effective stress management is called "positive affirmations," where you learn to turn down the volume of your ego's negative voice (which can so easily whittle away self-esteem) and replace the negative chatter with positive reinforcements which, in turn, help boost self-esteem. Using positive affirmations, particularly during times of duress, can help you gain composure and balance and not succumb to the internal voice of negative critic. It is thought that these affirmations unite both conscious and unconscious energies of thought to help accomplish a goal. Affirmations are a common practice among actors, artists, and in particular, athletes.

At the time I became involved with the U.S. biathlon team, it had been in existence for only about twenty-five years, a short time compared to the millennium that people in Scandinavian countries had been practicing this hunting practice-turned-sport. We Americans were lost babes in the snowy woods.

Of the six team members, a man named Raymond was a defector from the U.S.S.R. Raymond's presence definitely made for rather interesting team dynamics. In short, he had a defiant streak in him a mile wide, something I should have suspected from a defector—he didn't get where he was by placidly going along with authority. In my attempts to improve the athletes' mental skills, such as concentration, confidence, visualization, and team dynamics, I struck out again and again with Raymond. He turned a deaf ear to nearly all my endeavors—often cracking jokes and making snide comments under his breath, just loud enough for all to hear.

During my efforts to introduce the premise of positive affirmations, Raymond turned up his nose. Despite my best efforts, Raymond would have no part of it. On more than one occasion, he stuck his face close to mine and, with an air of defiance, said in a thick Latvian accent, "I don't believe in affirmation statement!" Then he would walk away in a huff.

When the world biathlon championships came to Lake Placid in 1987, the American team was in the best position in its history to have one of its members receive a medal.

I watched the race with much anticipation. In what looks like orchestrated chaos, hundreds of skiers, rifles strapped to their backs, cross the starting line, jockeying for position to take the lead for a ten-kilometer distance before they arrive at the shooting range, where they must fire five shots. Then they would ski off to repeat the process all over again three more times.

Raymond approached the range, grabbing the rifle off his back as he skied into his designated spot. Right as he took aim, he noticed that positioned next to him was a former Russian teammate. Remembering this athlete's skill, Raymond's confidence fell a few notches. Pondering his first shot, Raymond's attention then turned to a competitor on his other side, also a fellow Russian of equal standing. The pressure was on. Raymond, who was known for missing his first shot, aimed and fired. To his surprise, he hit it. He proceeded to clear the remaining four shots as well.

Back on the shooting range after another grueling trek around the ski course, Raymond cleared another five rounds. He became ecstatic, as did the entire American contingent. He did better than he had ever done before.

Soon after his race, Raymond skied up to where I was standing. With a smile from ear to ear, he looked me in the eye and said in a thick accent, "I have new affirmation statement!" A bit surprised, I inquired, "Congratulations! What is it?"

With as much pride as he could muster, he said under a puff of cold air, "I still got the goods!"

> Positive affirmations give balance to the negative airplay of the ego and make our lives more stress-free. You don't have to be a champion athlete to gain from the benefits of positive self-talk.

2

Simple Pleasures

I have had the privilege to stay in five-star resort hotels, dine at exclusive restaurants, and attend riveting rock concerts. But, to be honest, these experiences really can't compare to many of the greatest moments I've had which cost absolutely nothing. The other day, while I was out jogging by the creek, a little boy called me over to show me the collection of crawdads he had caught. His excitement was exhilarating. Hummingbirds at my feeder can brighten a dark and dreary morning. Watching a gaggle of Canadian geese pass overhead—in Colorado, a flock might number two hundred—has a way of vanquishing any remnants of sorrow I might have. In academic terms, these are referred to as "emotional uplifts." I just call them "simple pleasures."

Simple pleasures can best be described as those times when we find ourselves living in the present moment, enjoying its simplicity. So often our minds are preoccupied with past failures or future problems, leaving little or no time to enjoy the present. Simple pleasures are neither lavishly expensive nor incredibly time-consuming. They don't cause stress; they reduce it. It may be an overused phrase, but it's often true that the best things in life are free.

Ageless wisdom often reminds us of the universal law of attraction: whatever you set your mind on, you attract to yourself. Also called self-fulfilling prophecy, the law of attraction says that if you focus on negative things you will attract more negativity. Similarly, putting your attention on the positive will open your mind to a greater source of positive aspects to enjoy. That's what simple pleasures are all about—focusing on the positive side long enough to restore a sense of equilibrium to your life.

In teaching the concept of simple pleasures to my college students and workshop participants, I ask them to make a list of those simple things that bring them pleasure in an otherwise stressful day. Here are some of their answers:

1. When I get down in the dumps, I head to the nearest grocery store and start reading several greeting cards. I often find myself laughing out loud and this is definitely pleasurable.
2. Here is what I suggest. I suffer from SAD (seasonal affective disorder). My self-prescribed cure is to go to a florist greenhouse and smell the plants and flowers. This always puts me in a better mood.
3. Have you ever heard a recording of Ella Fitzgerald? Her voice is amazing. To hear her sing Cole Porter's "Night and Day" is a one-way ticket to heaven.
4. My favorite simple pleasure, and I have many, is to pick up the phone and call a friend. Sometimes we just talk, but more often than not we meet for

coffee or scones. With all this technology, I need real people contact. Friends are the best simple pleasures.

5. Go to a pet store. It's hard to feel bad when you're holding a cute puppy or kitten, even watching the goldfish is therapeutic. (I never have to worry about spending money because I can't have pets in my apartment.)
6. My suggestion is to fill the tub with hot water and add some bath oils, light a candle or two, turn off the lights, and soak. Sure works for me!
7. Some people may go shopping (as in retail therapy), but what I do is pack up items in my closet that have not been worn in a while and bring them to Goodwill. There is something about helping others that tends to lift my spirits.
8. My greatest simple pleasure is listening to music, and perhaps more so, hearing new music. I just discovered Dvorák's *Slavonic Dances*. Where have these been all my life? Opus 72, number 2 in E minor, is just incredible!
9. If I want to take my mind off some problems from either home or work, I fill the birdfeeder with birdseed and watch the chickadees and finches come in to eat. I think doing this reminds me of my childhood, which was pretty damn good by comparison to a lot of people's.
10. This simple pleasure cannot be done until a night with no cloud cover, but I pull a blanket out on the lawn and search for shooting stars and familiar constellations. It's amazing what can be found in

the night sky. Staring out in space always brings my problems back to a manageable size.

11. A single red rose in a bud vase does it for me every time, even if I buy it myself.
12. I take my car in to get washed. A clean car is heavenly and its pleasure just cannot be put into words.

A hot shower on a cold, wet day, a phone call from a dear friend, or the lick of a dog's tongue on your hand are reminders of life's simple pleasures. These delightful interludes not only pull us into the present moment, they also remind us to practice the art of gratitude. Each brief passage brings the mind and soul to a point of balance, and as such, gratitude comprises the last essential component of each simple pleasure.

> It doesn't take much to lift one's spirits: simple pleasures abound everywhere. All we need to do is prepare the mind, look, then enjoy.

3

Dinner with Merlin

Savoring the aroma and taste of delicious morsels of food is thought to be one of nature's best automatic relaxation techniques. That's because sensations that seduce the taste buds and massage the gastrointestinal tract also calm the central nervous system. Salmon à l'orange. Risotto. Swiss fondue. Crêpes. Strawberries. Chocolate. And, lest we forget—ice cream therapy. Food serves as a pacifier, a fact that both babies and mothers are well aware of, a habit that begins the moment we exit the womb and continues for many, many decades.

The art of eating does require an element of patience in order to relish the flavor and texture of each bite. Inhaling one's food, while an all-too-common practice, does not promote the relaxation response. And while a hectic day at work may dampen the romance of practicing the culinary arts at home, it is nothing that a night out on the town can't remedy. Remember the line in the Disney movie *Beauty and the Beast:* "When you're stressed, it's fine dining we suggest. Be our guest, be our guest, be our guest!"

Caught in the fast-paced lifestyle that we are all so

accustomed to, I am embarrassed to admit that eating fast, dare I say "wolfing" my food, is a behavior that I acquired in college. With the exception of eating in a classy restaurant, it is a habit that I found difficult to correct. That is, until I met Merlin, during the rite of passage called getting a family dog.

One look at Merlin and you know he comes from the species *canine lupine:* wolf. Merlin is not a first-generation timberwolf, but close enough to the original gene pool that once you meet him, you can skip a trip to Yellowstone National Park to get the feeling of dancing with this species. It would be fair to say that Merlin has a touch of husky and German shepherd, and perhaps it is this mix that cultivated, if not refined, his eating habits. He certainly doesn't wolf down his food.

We picked up Merlin at the animal shelter hours before he was destined to join Rip Van Winkle in Sleepy Hollow. One look in his eyes and you could tell he was ever so grateful. I have no doubt that animals know these things. They can smell death. We were told that he was a stray, about two years old, and from the looks of his protruding rib cage, mighty hungry.

In an attempt to bond with Merlin, I held him on my lap for the entire two-hour car trip home. Once inside the house, I gave him a bath and fed him, first with a few dog biscuits, then his own bowl of food.

Holding out a biscuit, Merlin first sniffed the peace offering and then ever so gently, opened his mouth and extending his tongue as if in slow motion, reached for the food, bringing the piece into his mouth. Then with the grace of royalty, began to chew, slowly. He looked up, making eye contact with me and in his own way saying "thanks." Moments later he walked over to his bowl and repeated this delicate, deliberate process with the food in his dish.

Later that evening Merlin joined us for dinner, again eating very slowly, chewing every bite before swallowing. I was stunned, because in all my exposure to dogs, I had never seen anything like this.

Eating is surely one of the finer aspects of life. Many people eat so fast, however, that they hardly taste what they place in their mouths before they gulp it down into the depths of their gastrointestinal tracks. Eating dinner with Merlin is a constant reminder to enjoy the simple pleasures of life.

> Perhaps it's rare that humans can learn positive behaviors from their pets, but I have learned something from Merlin—eat slowly, taste each piece of food in my mouth, and savor the flavor before I swallow. How relaxing!

4

Stepping Out of the Void

It is a misconception to think that human spirituality is the metaphorical equivalent of a trip to Disney World. While it is true that there are many joyous moments we associate with the journey of our lives, the stressful episodes are also part of the same voyage. The most difficult circumstances lead us to the edge of the void, what I refer to as the "emptying process," winter in the seasons of the soul. We have all been there. The void is where loss occurs, and its lesson is a difficult one. It is during this dark night of the soul that we are gently reminded to "be in this world, but not of it."

Ironically, when most people come to the precipice of the void, fear holds them back. They don't budge. But the nature of life is dynamic, not static. Energy must flow. I am convinced that if we do not move forward, we are first nudged, then pushed by some unseen, yet divine, force.

Let there be no doubt; the void contains moments of grief and sadness. To grieve a situation is not only normal, it's healthy. But prolonged grieving suffocates the soul. In times of stress, the emotion of pity is plentiful, but everything is relative. If there is a lesson to be learned through moments of loss, it is to grieve fully, and then move on. The dark night of the soul is only a night, not a lifetime. Just as winter turns to spring, so too does night become day.

Perhaps it's human nature, but our first response in the void is to want to fill it up in an attempt to give ourselves a sense of security. I think this is where the term "retail therapy" originates. Yet filling the void with material possessions or even addictive behaviors just results in spinning our wheels. Sage advice reminds us that to step out of the void, we must first step *into* it. In truth, the void is not the black pit of despair. It is really the womb of creation, what some call the realm of possibilities.

However, there comes a time when it's right to exit the void, to rejoin the world, hopefully a bit wiser. One of the best ways to take the first step out of the darkness of the grieving process into the light of a new day is to engage in service. To give of yourself to others in times of need, even when you feel there is nothing to give, lessens your own need for sympathy and evaporates self-pity.

A dynamic colleague of mine has an international reputation for bringing out the best in people. A leader in the human potential movement, Jean Houston has counseled kings, presidents, and corporate executives, as well as blue-collar workers and the poor. Not long ago, an episode of national acclaim, involving First Lady Hillary Clinton, was falsely exaggerated in the press, resulting in a tarnished image. What could have been a high point quickly became a crushing blow to her career. She lost several consulting offers and speaking engagements. The event became her dark night of the soul. The whole affair resulted in a significant period of time for deep self-reflection.

Left with much free time on her hands, Jean stepped back to look at the big picture, sized up her own potential, and pondered her options. In one of her conference workshops I attended, she shared these comments:

"I felt vulnerable," she explained. "But vulnerability led to availability and I decided to make myself available to those who were in a much worse situation than I. So I did some volunteer work with cancer and AIDS patients. I sat with them by their bedsides. I listened to their stories. I prayed, I laughed, I cried, and I smiled with them," she explained. "It was healing for all of us."

Service is a word that often falls on deaf ears, particularly in times of stress, but this need not be the case. While it may seem that in our own troubled times we have nothing to give anyone, the truth is that there is *always* someone we can be of service to, particularly as we emerge from the grieving process. The most effective teacher, therapist, or counselor is one who has been there. Empathy creates a sound foundation for genuine service.

> A line in Max Erhman's poem "Desiderata" reads, "For there are always greater and lesser persons than yourself. Strive to be happy." In times of stress we may turn our gaze to those whom we deem to be greater, and ask why do we have it so bad. Instead, we should count our blessings and share them as best as we can with those in greatest need.

5

The Glass *Is* Half-Full

So much of effective stress management is harnessing the winds of positive thought in a sea of negativity. In these days of rapid change, that's not always easy to do. Negative thoughts feed upon themselves, making mountains out of molehills. The end result distorts our vision: we see only gray clouds where there's also a deep blue sky. Worse, negative thoughts tend to attract more negative thoughts, turning gray clouds black and holding them overhead for a very long time.

Research studies reveal that an optimistic outlook on life is not only good for the mind, it's good for the body as well. Optimistic people are noted for getting fewer colds and flus than those hiding under a black anvil of thought. Moreover, unresolved negative thoughts suppress the immune system, setting the stage for illnesses far worse than the common cold. While perpetually viewing life through rose-colored glasses is considered by many to be a form of denial, relocating to the darker side of human emotions serves us no better. Optimism gives balance to moments of fear that can immobilize the human spirit. For this reason, optimism is essential to our health and well-being.

I have always considered myself an optimist. Perhaps, considering my background as a child of two alcoholic parents, people may wonder how this is so. Yet optimism was something I knew I had inside, and I continued to nurture it throughout my life, every step of the way. I experienced the power of positive thinking, from my dealings with a loan officer as I purchased my first house, to getting off with only a warning for a potentially expensive speeding ticket. Rose-colored glasses notwithstanding, optimism has gotten me through a lot of difficult situations.

As a young boy, I would often read the biographies and autobiographies of scientists, explorers, statesmen, and heroes. I learned that optimism was a common factor in their lives. In many cases, optimism paved the way on a rough and narrow course. I also learned that optimism is not a genetic characteristic. It is everyone's birthright, but it must be attended to or it will surely atrophy.

Optimism is spirit in motion; pessimism is spirit in constipation. I am of the opinion that everyone has the potential to be an optimist because I believe it is an inherent human trait. In the words of lyricist Johnny Mercer, all we have to do is "accentuate the positive" and eliminate the negative. This is step one in turning curses into blessings.

As an exercise for my students, I ask them to define the terms "optimist" and "pessimist," and then, as best they can, explain to me where they see themselves in the continuum. Here are some of their definitions of an optimist.

An optimist is:

- Someone who sees the positive, even in the worst of all situations.
- Someone who is carefree and seems to enjoy life without reservation.
- Someone who doesn't let failure limit their growth as a human being.
- Someone who can find redeeming qualities in just about everyone, even a pessimist.
- Someone who sees lots of clouds in the sky and describes the day as mostly sunny.
- Someone who takes a personal setback as only a *temporary* inconvenience.
- Someone who counts their blessings instead of their misfortunes.
- Someone who loses a job and says there is a better one waiting.
- Someone who has the ability to reevaluate their expectations so as not to become depressed when they fall short.
- Someone who is generally happy and who is nice to be around.
- Someone who takes things in stride, is able to enjoy themselves, and is able to adapt to the situation at hand.
- Someone who sees things clearly and accepts what is or what cannot be changed and doesn't spend time fighting it.

- Someone who continually explores new areas of life, and who can accept others who are different from them as unique.
- Someone who has enough faith in themselves to see themselves through a crisis.
- Someone who describes a pessimist as a person with potential.

Roses have both beautiful petals and piercing thorns. Where do you choose to place your attention?

6

Grandmother McNulty

I have a tradition when I begin my first class of the semester or a weekend workshop, where fostering a sense of camaraderie is paramount to the success of the class. The tradition is in the form of an icebreaker, a question that invites students to do a little soul-searching. Then, one by one, we share the answers and reveal a little bit about ourselves to initiate the connection process. One question I often ask is this: What person outside of your parents and siblings has been the greatest influence in your life?

One reason for asking this question deals with the self-esteem. In all my years of teaching stress management, I have come to learn that high self-esteem is the foundation upon which all other stress coping skills and relaxation techniques rest. While there are many theories of self-esteem, one that I have been attracted to is the idea that self-worth is comprised of four aspects: uniqueness, empowerment, social support, and role models.

This particular icebreaker honors the concept of role models. What I typically find is that the basis of each person's answer ties directly to the notion of love. Indeed, love is the greatest and most lasting influence in every person's life.

Although I have been influenced by a great many people, from schoolteachers and college professors to humanitarians, one person who comes to mind every time is my maternal grandmother. The youngest of nine children, she was the sole surviving member of her family's generation. From as long as I can remember, there was a quality of dignity about her. I grew up hearing countless stories of her colorful past, thinking how great it was to be related to her.

Her father was a secretary to President McKinley, and stories abound of her playing as a young girl at the White House, even sitting on the president's lap. She told me that she was asked out to a movie on her first date. When she and her escort walked out of the theater, news broke that the Titanic had sunk. In high school I learned that her uncle was killed at the Battle of Little Big Horn with General Custer (talk about stress!). She was born before women had the right to vote, but once that amendment passed, she never missed an election.

My grandmother lived in an age when national celebrations included ticker-tape parades for celebrities such as Charles Lindbergh—which she watched from the grandstand—and national mournings, including those for Presidents McKinley and John F. Kennedy. I once asked her why she didn't like to fly and she told me that when she was quite young, she saw the Wright brothers ride their plane over the Potomac river. "I wasn't impressed then, and I'm not impressed now," she told me with a slight smirk.

These and other historical moments were fascinating,

but it was her compassion and grace in everyday life that made the deepest impression on me. My grandmother had seen much change—from the Wright brothers to the first space shuttle—and weathered great difficulty in her life. Yet through it all, she held her head high and always kept her heart open to those around her.

One day I arrived at her apartment to find the door ajar. She was crying and badly shaken. As she turned to greet me, I saw blood dripping from her forehead. I then learned that she had just returned home from a quick trip to the grocery store, in anticipation of my visit. Halfway between the store and her apartment, she had been robbed and thrown to the ground by two teenagers. A trip to the hospital revealed a concussion and two broken ribs. That evening, my grandmother put it all in perspective.

"I'll be OK," she reassured me. "I have been through a lot worse. I don't know what makes people do that. They must need the money quite badly." Harboring no grudge, she steered the conversation toward me and my first year at college. Getting up to make some tea, she smiled. "They might have stolen some money, but they did leave the groceries. Can I fix you some dessert?"

I was not only greatly influenced by her but deeply inspired by her as well.

> Actor Sir Laurence Olivier once said, "Legends are made up of ordinary people who do extraordinary things." May the legend live within all of us.

7

That Special Something...

I do several exercises on the topic of self-esteem in my stress management workshops, because when self-esteem is high, problems tend to roll off your back, whereas when self-esteem is low you become a magnetic bull's-eye for the negative impact of daily stressors. One particular exercise regards the aspect of uniqueness, an essential component of high self-esteem.

We each have a gift or unique quality that makes us special. Moments of stress, when the ego is caught in a downward spiral of self-defeating thoughts, can disempower our unique attributes. At worst, we lose track of our particular gifts and feel we aren't worthy of anything.

That's why I love this exercise, which requires each person to list five attributes which make him or her special. Typically, when I first give this assignment I am greeted with long stares and oppressive silence. The silence continues as people stall to come up with even one item on their list.

As a rule, people focus on their weaknesses, not their strengths. Ironically, those things which we see as our imperfections are often viewed by others as rare jewels. To illustrate the point and get people thinking, I tell workshop participants this story:

I was in Lake Placid, New York, for the biathlon world championships. As one of two sport psychologists, I had been working diligently with the six-member Olympic team to refine their mental training skills for the big event. Three years of relaxation techniques, positive affirmations, visualizations, mental rehearsal, goal-setting, and team dynamics have been set in motion for this one day of competition.

On this particular day, the weather was ideal for racing. Cool but not freezing; sunny but not windy. The athletes were primed for the "home court" advantage. I walked off the field, heading toward the lodge to warm up by the woodstove and sip a cup of hot chocolate. Inside the lodge, several athletes were waxing their skis and a few officials were attending to some last-minute details. Standing by the fire, I was approached by Chip, a seasoned veteran of the U.S. Olympic team. Chip's imposing height was disarmed by his smile, a feature commonly found on his face.

"Great day for a race, huh, Chip?" I inquired.

"I guess," he answered. Then he paused and looked down at the ground. "You know I've been bothered by something and I've been wanting to talk to you. Is this a good time?" he asked.

"Sure," I answered, thinking he might want to review some mental training tips.

"You know, I just get the impression that women don't think I'm attractive. I have these real thin lips and when I smile I've got these huge dimples."

My first impulse was to laugh out loud, thinking: you've got to be kidding, you've got a world champion race in a half an hour and you're thinking of this? My next thought was, I have failed in my mission to help the team win a medal. But rather than react, I responded with this comment: "Chip, listen, let's talk about this later. I promise! Right now I want you to focus on the race. Get psyched, rehearse your technique in your mind, OK?" I gripped his shoulder and gave a good squeeze, then patted him on the back as he turned for the door. "Good luck," I yelled.

Moments later, just as I drank the last drop of cocoa, a young, attractive woman approached me.

"Hi," she said, "was that Chip, the Olympian, you were just talking to?"

I wasn't sure I wanted to admit it, but I nodded my head yes.

"Oh," she continued, "he is so cute, so handsome! He has the thinnest lips and I just love it when he smiles, cause he has the cutest dimples." Rolling her eyes back, she sighed.

I stared at her, nearly in shock.

"Quick," I yelled, "go tell him!"

Leo Buscaglia, author of a great many books on love, often spoke on the nature of self-love. Until we learn to accept ourselves with all our pluses and minuses, he explained, we cannot love ourselves unconditionally. Buscaglia referred to uniqueness as the X-factor.

So, what are your unique attributes? Your special qualities? Your X-factor? This is where your strength lies. If you are having a hard time coming up with any, try focusing on your points of weakness, and ask some trusted friends what traits they admire in you—you'll be surprised!

> Within everyone is a rare precious gem. When we scrape off the ego's dirt and grime we shine.

8

Friends in Need

Imagine living a life in total isolation. It's not possible. By nature, human beings are social animals. While it's nice to have a moment or two to yourself, complete independence gets old after a while, and lonely. Undeniably, we are all connected. In the words of John Dunne, "No man is an island"—nor should we try to be.

Studies show that under increasing personal and professional demands, prolonged periods of isolation lower our sense of self-esteem and increase our stress exponentially. Common sense would indicate (and research bears out) that keeping company with friends tends to take the edge off a bad day, a bad week, or, for that matter, a bad life. Medical science hasn't figured out exactly how this works. Some credit the endorphin response, while newer research suggests it has something to do with the human energy field. Regardless, it appears that sharing our problems with friends and being in the physical presence of those who support us (even if they don't always agree with us) dissipates the negative effects of stress.

In academic circles this is known as the buffer principle. To the average person on the street, it is known as a friend in need. Just like the tablets one takes to relieve (buffer) the buildup of acid in the gastrointestinal track, friends neutralize the toxic effect of stress. Misery loves company—for company, it seems, dilutes misery to tolerable levels.

Perhaps the most amazing evidence of the buffer theory was shown by Dr. David Spiegel, a faculty member of Stanford University's School of Medicine. Chagrined by the claims of Dr. Bernie Siegel's work with cancer patients, and often confused for him due to the similarity of their last names, Spiegel set out to prove Siegel wrong. His hypothesis: support groups did not prolong the life of patients with metastatic breast cancer. To Spiegel's surprise, however, he found that those women who participated regularly in a patient support group lived, on average, five years longer than those who did not.

Statistics and number-crunching may satisfy the clinical bean-counters, but stories are the proof in the pudding.

Michelle is the director of Prestige Plus, a seniors program at Longmont United Hospital in Boulder County, Colorado. Originally created as an offsite health care program, it has become the local support group for over two thousand area seniors. Much of Michelle's job is to organize various health screenings for her members, although lately, due to their interest in alternative medicine, she has also begun integrating massage therapy, acupuncture, reflexology, and herbal remedies into the program services. Occasionally when a member goes into the hospital, Michelle will make a visit to see how he or she is doing.

"One day, I went to see Alice, who was dying of cancer.

Many times these people have no families, or they live too far away to visit. For some members, I am their family. I sat there with her for a while visiting, and then she turned to me and said, 'Michelle, I'd like to be held. Would you hug me? When you have cancer, no one wants to touch you. But we need touch like everyone else.'"

Michelle didn't skip a beat. She climbed up into the hospital bed and gave Alice a long, loving embrace. Then the tears rolled down Michelle's face.

"I thought I was doing her a favor, but the truth is, I needed the hug as much as she did," she said.

It wasn't a hug that surprised Ian O'Gorman, but nonetheless he was amazed. Ian was diagnosed with cancer around the time of his tenth birthday. He was warned that the chemotherapy treatment might make his hair fall out, and it did. To avoid the embarrassment of looking like a Cabbage Patch kid, he decided to have his head shaved. When he was well enough to attend school, he walked into his classroom to see his teacher and all his buddies with their heads shaved, too!

Sometimes the littlest gesture of friendship can have an extraordinary impact, as evidenced in a letter I received a while ago.

> Dear Luke,
>
> You probably don't remember me, so let me give you a hint. I was the guy with ALS (Lou Gerhig's Disease) who approached you in Houston while you were giving a presentation some time ago. Thank you for your kindness and generosity in mailing me a book. I apologize for not writing to you sooner to thank you. Shortly after I received your gift, my brother was killed in an accident and this is just one

of the few problems I am trying to deal with along with my illness. Right now I am focusing on my wife and three kids, and keeping life as normal as possible for them. Man, I tell you, I know you have heard the saying, when it rains, it pours. Well I can tell you I don't think there is any facet of my life that is not being tested right now.

I want you to know that in times like these, it's those things, like what you did, that keeps a person with hope and the ability to face another day.

Sincerely,
Randy

Friends in need are friends indeed. Be a good friend to someone in need. You will be paid back immeasurably.

9

Christmas Lights

Joanne wanted to be a mother from the moment she got her first doll for Christmas when she was five years old. But it would be many decades later, including eight years of marriage, when she finally got the news from her physician—yes, she was pregnant. Joanne was elated! She wasted no time getting ready for *the* day. Anyone who knows Joanne will tell you that assertiveness is one of her strengths; it's how she exhibits empowerment. From Lamaze classes and parenting seminars to relaxation tapes, she did everything in her power to give her baby the warmest welcome to Planet Earth.

Sometime toward the end of her sixth month, the course of events changed slightly. One night after fixing supper, Joanne went upstairs to the bathroom before heading to bed. Looking down on the bathroom floor, Joanne saw blood everywhere. "Call the doctor," she screamed to her husband. In what seemed like only moments later, with her husband driving at light-speed toward the hospital, Joanne felt a kick, enough to know that her little miracle was still alive.

"As they whisked me up to Labor and Delivery, the bleeding had stopped and I thought somewhat naively that everything was fine," Joanne explained. "As it turned out, I was in labor. They gave me medications to try and stop the contractions and I used what I had learned about relaxation and went to sleep just after one o'clock," she said.

The next morning the hemorrhaging began again and this time the decision was made for her to have a cesarean immediately. Joanne awoke in the recovery room to learn that her baby daughter was in critical, but stable, condition. Wednesday, December 8, 1976, the world welcomed Michelle Annelee West.

Because Joanne's hemorrhaging was so bad, she was confined to bed for three days, unable to see the baby she longed to hold. Taking a deep breath, she affirmed to herself that when the time was right, she would be reunited with her child. Meanwhile, a team of physicians broke the news to her and her husband that the baby's chance of survival was less that 50 percent. Again Joanne affirmed her belief and placed the outcome in God's hands.

Two days later, on Friday evening, December 10, Joanne made it to the intensive care nursery to see Michelle for the first time. A collapsed lung kept the "premie" on a respirator. Joanne could only stroke her with a few fingers, yet the contact was energizing and the love from her heart was immense. She smiled constantly with confidence at her daughter.

"I had Catholic friends lighting candles, Buddhist friends singing chants, and every nurse in intensive care pulling for her. I knew she was going to make it. I nicknamed her 'Sam' for 'small adorable miracle.' Miracles do happen and Michelle certainly was a miracle by everyone's estimation." Drawing on faith, hope, and love, Joanne prayed like she never had before. This is one way she empowers herself.

Empowerment is the last of the four pillars of high self-esteem. Many people confuse empowerment for control, but they are not the same thing. Control involves ego. It employs manipulation and often deceit. Control is fear acted out. On the other hand, empowerment is the realization of personal strength and the cultivation of inner resources. Whereas control is akin to giving your power away, by thinking that you can control others (the illusion of control), empowerment is reclaiming your personal sovereignty even when what's ahead appears to be a dead-end. Empowerment is knowing you have a can-do attitude and letting that positive energy flow. In her situation, there was absolutely nothing, no final outcome, that Joanne could control. Yet empowerment was her ace in the hole, and she played this card every day.

As days passed into weeks, "Sam" got off all machines, but she was still too little to leave the hospital. More than anything, Joanne wanted to have her baby home for Christmas. The team of physicians warned her that Michelle, born so premature, would have to stay in intensive care for several more weeks. Honoring their expertise, she affirmed her desire to be together as one family.

On Christmas Eve, Joanne made her daily visit to the hospital to see her daughter, secretly hoping that Michelle would go home with her. It appeared, however, that Michelle's first "real" Christmas would have to wait.

"There was only one nurse in the unit due to a low census," Joanne explained. "She saw me holding back the tears and tried to comfort me."

"What do you mean, no Christmas!" the nurse exclaimed. "You must be kidding. Joanne, we have Christmas in this room every day," said the nurse. "Just look around the room, look at all these babies. Isn't Christmas about little babies? Isn't Christmas about God's love? Isn't Christmas about miracles? Some of these babies have no medical reason to be alive right now, save a miracle. Christmas—why we have it every day in this room!" At this point she hit the light switch for a moment and the room succumbed to darkness, save for hundreds of red and green lights from all the monitors. Christmas lights.

As it turned out, another miracle happened that Christmas Day. Joanne and her husband received a phone call from the hospital. Little Michelle was strong enough to leave. They could come and take her home. So they drove to the hospital, picked up Michelle, and home they went.

That evening, at her sister's house, with the living room lights off, Joanne sat in a chair in front of the fire holding her small little miracle. She glanced over at the tiny lights on the Christmas tree.

"Tears of joy welled up in my eyes," she said, "as I realized what Christmas lights really are."

> Empowerment isn't a gift, it is a birthright. Yet, like a living plant, it must be nurtured and cultivated to grow. The source of power comes from within, yet manifests as assertiveness through our thoughts and actions. When you think of someone who appears to have little or no stress, you are viewing empowerment.

10

The Burlington Book Club

Burlington, Vermont, is a small city that sits on the pristine shores of Lake Champlain. The lake is over 130 miles long, starting deep in New York State and emptying into Canada's St. Lawrence Seaway. Perhaps because of its length and the boundary between Vermont and New York, Lake Champlain is affectionately called the "west coast" of New England. Due to what the Weather Channel calls the "lake effect," Burlington has a lot of cloudy days. You can go the whole month of February and never see the sun. So what do people do in a town like Burlington on cold, rainy days or snowy evenings? They read lots of books.

Not long after I moved to Burlington in 1987 to work with the Olympic biathlon team, I met Laurie through a mutual friend. Laurie is a vivacious character who knows practically everybody in the state of Vermont, most likely all of New England, and quite possibly the entire world. It is not an understatement to say that she is extremely well-connected, and knows the importance of making and keeping good friends. She didn't actually coin the term "support group," but she might as well have. She definitely appreciates the value of connectedness.

When you move to a new area, feelings of loneliness and isolation are not uncommon. New friendships, and old acquaintances, if you are lucky enough to have them, are crucial to your health. Because health is so inextricably linked to self-esteem and self-esteem is enhanced by social support, support groups—book clubs, single parent clubs, Alcoholics Anonymous groups, or summer softball teams—constitute one cornerstone of any successful stress management program.

The Burlington Book Club was one of many of Laurie's ideas to foster a sense of camaraderie among friends. It wasn't long after I met her that I was invited to join. And it wasn't much longer before I realized that reading wasn't really a criteria for maintaining club membership.

My invitation to join the club was extended over lunch one day. As we walked inside the restaurant on the shores of Lake Champlain, a waiter came right over to us, kissed Laurie on the cheek, made a comment about the cloudy weather, then showed us to our table. As we sat down, the owners came over and greeted Laurie with a hug.

"Everyone is so friendly here," Laurie said (I was to realize over the course of many months that it was she who cast a huge net of friendship over the region). Once we had ordered, the book club became the focus of our conversation.

"We meet the first Tuesday of each month. I'm not sure what the book selection is this month. I am so far behind in my reading, but it doesn't matter. Just come. Oh, yeah. It's a potluck, so bring something to eat. It doesn't matter. Anything will be OK."

Curious about the club's format and history, and wanting to make a decent appearance, I followed up with some questions. "Laurie, thanks," I said, "Now what types of books do you guys normally read? Novels, science fiction, autobiographies?"

"Well, it varies, really. Someone makes a suggestion and...oh, you'll see. It's pretty casual," she explained. Then she paused for a moment, looked out the window at a sailboat, waived at the crew, then brought her attention back to the conversation.

"Everyone has become so busy that we have gotten in the habit of picking books that have been made into movies. That way, if you don't have time to read, you can rent the video. I do this all the time. Let's see, I think next month's book is *Out of Africa,* or is it *Dancing With Wolves?* I forget. It doesn't really matter.

"This is a very stress-free book club, right up your alley," she continued. "There is no obligation to actually read books. It's just an excuse to get together and visit. Sometimes no one has read the book we selected and we end up talking the whole night about politics, cross-country skiing, Hawaii, or something."

Our attention was redirected to a couple walking into the restaurant. They immediately came over to our table and greeted Laurie.

"Do you know everyone?" I asked, smiling, as the couple walked away.

"No, this is a small town, it just seems that way. You'll make lots of friends too. Just wait and see. Now, can you make next Tuesday night? It's a lot of fun."

Indeed, the Burlington Book Club lived up to its reputation. It fostered a sense of friendship, which is what good support groups do. It didn't take me long to realize that although books were the primary vehicle to get everyone together, it was the sense of belonging, the sense of connectedness, that was the real driving force which kept it going.

> Good friendships are paramount to high self-esteem and good health. A sense of belonging is an essential coping technique for stress. If you don't have a strong support group, start a book club (or a CD club, or...) as a catalyst for connectedness.

11

One Person Can Make a Difference

A pebble thrown into a still pond will not make a huge wave, but it will make a ripple, which then reverberates outward till it reaches the edge of the shore. Like pebbles, we too have such an effect. With six billion people on the planet, it may seem as if each life is infinitesimal in its meaning, yet each person is essential to the whole and each holds the potential for greatness. Significant and lasting changes don't require huge committees or mythical heroes. All that's required is love.

In summer 1998, at an Institute of Noetic Sciences conference in Kansas City, I stood upon the metaphorical shores of humanity and was touched by the ripple of one such pebble.

Balbir Mathur was raised in Allahabad, India, one of five children. The son of an army officer, Balbir came to the United States in 1958, with only six dollars in his pocket, to study business at Wichita State University. He must have learned his academic lessons well, for within a short time he became a successful business executive, traveling all over of the world.

It was on one such trip, while flying over the Mediterranean, gazing out the window at the island of Cypress, that Balbir had what he calls a "mystical experience." What began as a conversation with God became a lifelong mission.

"Someone—in a voice I do not understand, nor can fully describe—asked me what I saw as I looked down. High above the earth I saw extremes and opposites: light and dark, hope and despair, wealth and poverty. It was after this moment that I began to have a pain in my finger. Soon the pain invaded my whole body. Unable to walk, I eventually became bedridden."

For two years, Balbir was immobilized with pain. All he could do was rest and eat. A suggestion by his sister prompted him to fast for several days. Denying himself the only pleasure he could enjoy, he began to fast from both food and water. On the fifth day a miracle occurred. Balbir experienced a vision of trees. At that moment, he knelt and dedicated his life to alleviating world hunger. He arose out of bed and went for a five-mile walk, as if he had never been sick. He knew he was healed.

But life did not become easier for Balbir. He lost all interest in his business. Family savings disappeared. There was no income. "I was in an awkward place," Balbir explained. "I had left one shore, but had not yet arrived at another." Guided by unseen forces, Balbir raised his sails to catch the winds of grace. Once again they led him across the Atlantic.

Within a month's time, Balbir took a trip to Zimbabwe as a delegate to an African-American conference. There the mystical voice returned, whispering in his ear a name that would repeat itself for three days: "Johnny Appleseed." Balbir got the message. He canceled the remainder of his itinerary and returned to his mother's home in India to formulate his plan. He would plant 100 trees from the seeds of a lemon tree in his mother's yard. Why a lemon tree? As it turns out, Balbir had made a secret promise to the tree as a child, that one day he would plant a hundred trees from its seeds. The time had come to honor the promise.

With the blessing of a local healer, Balbir distributed the lemon saplings. Those who took a sapling promised in turn to plant eighteen more trees each to keep the legacy strong. Back in the States, his mission really took root when a group of eighth-graders in Wichita, Kansas, upon hearing his story, raised money for 103 fruit trees in India.

Today Balbir, with his wife, Treva, head a volunteer organization out of Wichita called Trees for Life, a self-help movement involving millions of people. Through their efforts, trees have been planted in Balbir's native India, in Guatemala, and in Brazil, supplying nutrient-rich fruit to community villages.

A week after first observing Balbir accept the Temple Award for Creative Altruism at the Noetic Sciences conference, the winds of grace brought him to Boulder, Colorado, where we met for lunch. There Balbir shared more of himself with me.

"I must say this experience was long in the making. A series of events took place that led up to it. At each step I merely agreed to move forward. I was terrified, but I said yes anyway. And yes, life became very tough after that. It tested every single fiber within me. My family and all my relationships were put to an extreme test. This is very important for people to understand. Otherwise they may think that visions solve all problems. In our culture, we seek fast results. The reality is just the reverse. Visions simply open the door to new horizons, and one cannot escape paying the full price.

"This is really a story of transformation. Perhaps the only reason I allow this intimate aspect of my life to be shared is because it is not just my story. In one way, it is the story of each and every one of us. Perhaps those who read it may get the courage to say yes when their time comes," Balbir said. There he repeated the closing comments he had shared upon receiving his award: "I do not wish to change God's world, that would be arrogant. What I do is an act of worship. How does one quantify worship? We really do not plant trees, we plant love, one tree at a time."

> One person *can* make a difference. The deed need not be monumental in scope, nor brilliant in fashion. As we assist those in need, we too share in the harvest of celebration.

section seven

Going with the Flow

THERE IS AN OLD PROVERB: "You cannot push water uphill." A simple message, yet we often question this wisdom and try to fight the currents of life's river, only to end up exhausted.

If each human journey can be described as a passage on the river of life, then it is fair to say that hope and confidence are the oars with which we paddle to navigate the shoals of stress. Sometimes the rapids are exhilarating, occasionally harrowing. At times placid waters are a welcome respite, at times they don't quite hit our threshold. Regardless, each and every time, we must remember to go with the flow and expect the best outcome. The following stories offer insights into the process of releasing expectations and taming the ego—in short, of moving like water.

1

No Time for a Flat Tire

Oh, if only it were a perfect world. But, then again, a perfect world would be boring and perhaps quite predictable. So often we wish we could control everything in our lives, yet the simple truth is that we can't. Relinquishing the illusion of control goes a long way toward eliminating stress in our lives and empowering us to take what action we can. It is a lesson we must remind ourselves of daily. In hindsight, it is often said, everything is perfect, most likely because the past cannot be changed or controlled. It can only be appreciated. Take a flat tire . . . please!

If you are going to drive from Denver to Vail, Colorado, there is really only one way to go: Interstate 70. Often called the ski resort highway, I-70 is one of the most scenic interstates in the country. This is the road that Bill and his wife Margerie took to Vail one summer afternoon. Bill was to be the keynote speaker at a sales conference, and even though he and his wife had been to Vail before, this time seemed special. There was magic in the air. As they exited off the highway and headed into Vail Village, Bill leaned over and gave his wife a kiss at the stop sign, whispering the words, "I love you."

After they checked in and freshened up, the couple took a walk outside to admire the Alpine view. More than once, Bill stopped along the banks of a nearby stream and after taking deep breaths of the fresh mountain air, told Margerie how great it was to be alive.

The conference started early the next morning and Bill's presentation was extremely well received, so much so that the question and answer period was extended, making Bill late for his departure back to the airport. During the last break, Margerie checked out, put their luggage in the rental car, and waited in the parking lot for her husband, the car motor running.

Due to the time crunch, the ride back to Denver, which normally takes about two hours, became a marathon of sorts. The two were scheduled to fly back to the East Coast in time for another conference the following day. If things went according to plan, it would work out, but there wasn't much room to play with in the schedule. So when a loud rumbling noise started to come from the left rear side of the car, Bill became worried. He knew immediately what it was—a flat tire. Pulling the car over, the thought occurred to him that this would be a ten-minute stop. They could still make it. It wasn't until he got all the luggage out of the trunk that he discovered that the spare tire was also flat. At this point, there was no way they were going to make their flight out of Denver. Margerie said she could see steam coming out of Bill's ears. Raising his hand to the sky, Bill gave God the finger.

Within twenty minutes, a truck pulled up and offered to take the couple to the nearest garage. An hour later, Bill and Margerie pulled out of the gas station and headed to the airport in hope of catching the next available flight.

At this point, Margerie decided to turn the radio on and listen to the news. What they heard made them pull over to the side of the road once again. A jet bound for Chicago from Denver had crashed in a cornfield in Iowa. The radio announcer repeated the airline flight number. Bill's wife pulled the tickets out of the envelope and gasped. "That was our flight," she said.

Bill stared out past the windshield for a moment and then quickly turned around to give Margerie a hug. Then he opened the door and stepped outside and looked up. The initial curse he had silently flung at the God who flattened car tire(s) now became a prayer of gratitude.

> We are instruments in the symphony of life, and God is the composer and conductor. Now and then we may play a solo and march to a different beat, but there is an inherent tempo and rhythm to all life which we must honor.

2

Dinner in a Noisy Restaurant

By all accounts, embarrassment is a significant stressor. After all, who wants to be the focus of attention, the butt of endless ridicule? No one! Yet sometimes it is just unavoidable, particularly in our youth. The three most embarrassing moments in a child's life, all of which might take place in school, are: walking around with your fly open (for guys!); vomiting in front of your friends; and dropping your tray in the school cafeteria. The first may elicit a few giggles, the last typically elicits a round of applause from all those who witnessed the event, as your face mirrors the color of a cooked lobster.

The ambiance of The Grill, a popular Denver eatery, looks nothing like a grade-school cafeteria, but it does have a few things in common with one, most notably the applause when something hits the floor. I learned this not long ago while eating lunch there. As I dove my fork into a pile of bowtie pasta, I looked up to see a waiter across the room bump into a customer and lose his grip on some dishes he had just cleared. *Boom! Bam! Crash!*

Now, typically when this happens in a restaurant, a hush can be heard as the last pieces of glass hit the floor. Perhaps even a few gasps. Never applause. But not at this restaurant. Within seconds, the entire staff of food servers broke out in a round of cheers and applause. I was astonished. Another spill happened again a few minutes later, and I could have sworn that this time it was intentional.

As my waiter came by with my dessert, I inquired about the unique response to dropping dishes. He said, "You see, the philosophy here is to have a good time. Waiting on tables can be very stressful, especially when it's really busy. So, with the encouragement of the management, as a means to reduce our stress, every now and then someone drops a plate or cup. It's a signal to others on the staff to lighten up. Of course when it's an accident, it's even better. Overall, it's a great stress reliever. Here, check this out," as I watched astounded, he tossed a plate on the floor. A thunderous round of applause soon followed. My server took a Broadway bow. All I could do was laugh.

> There is an expression that says, "Angels can fly because they take themselves lightly." When we do the same, we allow our spirits to soar.

3

Relieving Road Rage

When I get into my car, one of the first things I do is shove a tape in the cassette player and turn up the volume. I have several favorite tapes; one is a mix I made myself called "Passport to Ecstasy," which is comprised of songs from around the globe—Canada, Europe, Africa, Asia, Hawaii, Brazil, and Jamaica. Driving to the airport, this tape gets me in the mood for travel. It's an hour's drive from my house to Denver's new airport, during non-rush hour times; in highway traffic, it can take as long as ninety minutes. Music calms my nerves on the drive. Sometimes I see people in other cars putting on make-up or shaving, or eating something while talking on a cell phone, and I am amazed that there aren't even more accidents on our nation's highways. I hear that cars of the future will have fax machines and microwave ovens in the dashboard. My favorite bumper sticker these days is, "Hang up and drive."

Psychological studies show that if you put a small number of rats in a cage, more than likely they will all get along. But if the space for each rat decreases as more rats are forced to cohabitate, tension begins to mount. Each rat defends his or her own physical space; the overcrowded conditions lead to frustration and soon fighting occurs. The end result is that some rats die off. Perhaps it comes as no surprise that in many ways, rats and humans are very much alike. Lately, the rat race is becoming more like a rat fight in an overcrowded cage, particularly when people get behind the steering wheels of their cars.

Today, road rage has become the rage on the nation's highways. What was once known as something that could only happen in California, such as drive-by shootings, has now spread eastward—clear to the Atlantic seaboard.

Even Colorado, a state known for its laid-back citizens and polite drivers, is no longer immune to the problems of road rage. With over two million people driving to and from work in the Denver Metro area, frustrations hit an all-time record in summer 1997. A task force was created to examine the situation. A recommendation was made to place more police on the roads, hoping to minimize raging tempers. It was rumored that people were getting tickets for flipping the bird and cutting off motorists without the proper use of a signal.

Governor Roy Romer came up with his own idea as well. In an effort to bring peace to the mountain state, Romer suggested to Colorado drivers that rather than raising the middle finger as a nonverbal gesture of hostility, they raise *two* fingers and give the peace symbol instead. It really does work!

> In a moment of frustration, remember: two fingers are better than one!

4

The Reluctant Nurse

Before Western medicine became obsessed with diagnostic technology, the foundation of nursing consisted primarily of "tender loving care." The advances of modern medicine have been nothing less than phenomenal, yet this aspect of holistic caregiving has often been neglected, much to the detriment of patient care in general. Given the chance, nurses from Maine to California will tell you they spend more time monitoring screens and filling out forms than attending to the specific needs of their patients.

At the same time that advances in technology raced into the hospitals, there has been a resurgent interest in the ageless wisdom of healing, holistic healing which accesses and influences the human energy field. Energy medicine suggests that human beings are comprised of layers of energy, the most dense layer being the physical body. By and large, these layers of energy are undetectable by the human eye, but throughout the ages there have been those who claim to be able to see the layers of the human energy field, which they describe as layers of consciousness. Physicists call this phenomenon the human energy field. Shamans, healers, and sages refer to them as auras. These same wisdom-keepers tell us that love is the greatest healing energy, bringing harmony and balance to the emotional, mental, and spiritual layers in the human energy field.

In the early seventies, two nurses, Dora Kuntz and Dolores Krieger, synthesized several esoteric aspects of energy healing into a systematic style which they called Therapeutic Touch. For over twenty-five years, the Therapeutic Touch technique has been taught all over the country to nurses as a complementary form of healing in hospital settings. Moreover, although the exact dynamics are not understood by modern Western scientific thought, there have been several clinical studies which document the effectiveness of TT as a therapeutic healing modality. The premise of TT is the healing power of love.

When new ideas (or, as in this case, old concepts that have been revisited) emerge, they may be perceived as threatening to those who, at best, are attached to old ways of thinking. Such was the case with the head nurse at a midwest hospital. When she learned that several of her staff were enrolled in a course in Therapeutic Touch, she was outraged. "That stuff is quackery! Hocus-pocus! Nonsense," she yelled. A woman quite attached to her ego, she forbade any of her staff to attend the workshop, threatening reprisal. Staff members went anyway. When the group of nurses came back to work the next day, they saw a sign posted on the entrance to the hospital: "There will be no healing in this hospital."

> The biggest roadblock on the journey of life is our own ego. When we encounter an obstacle on our

own life-journey, let us first turn within to begin to dismantle it.

5

The Priest and the Snake

Most of us know that stress produces the fight or flight response. What we tend to forget is that anger is the emotion that fuels the "fight" part of the response (fear drives flight). That's why anger has not received adequate press over the years. It's normal and even healthy to feel brief moments of anger—it's a natural reaction to stress.

It is said that the average American gets angry at least fifteen times a day. If that number seems high to you, you're not alone. Many people simply ignore these feelings. Perhaps because of the extreme violence associated with anger, we are taught by our parents and teachers not to feel or express our anger. The result, however, can be quite damaging, as the body becomes the battlefield for the war games of the mind. Suppressed anger can result in several physical problems, from migraine headaches and ulcers to TMJ and hypertension.

Current studies on anger reveal that most people don't express anger very well. Actually, we do it rather poorly. We either stuff our frustration, or explode with vengeance. In the end, we either abuse ourselves or manipulate others, neither of which is healthy or productive. Venting anger is thought to be good as long as you vent to the person who angers you; otherwise venting simply validates your anger and the process repeats itself. Exercise, diplomatic communication, and refinement of expectations (every episode of anger is the result of unmet expectations) are three good ways to creatively release angry feelings. But first and foremost, we have to learn to recognize our anger, then honestly validate it.

As a child, I was taught not to show anger. The famous Irish temper notwithstanding, I was raised to keep up a happy disposition. Later I learned just how toxic to the body this can be, and I began to learn to feel and creatively express my anger. Sometimes, when the moment calls for it, all one needs to do is simply say, "I'm angry." Then let it go. In fact, just saying the words helps you to let it go. Here is one of my favorite stories about the benefits of anger.

In a remote village at the foot of the Himalayas, where the pine trees of the foothills meet the palms of the rainforest, there was a monk who studied to become a priest. Upon ordination, he was given a plot of land by his elders and, with money borrowed from his father, he built a glorious temple. Finely crafted and ornately decorated, the temple took him five years to complete. Because he was so well liked, friends would donate proceeds from their crops, but surprisingly none assisted him in the completion of the temple.

On the day the building was completed, he hiked the four-mile path to town and posted a proclamation announcing the opening of his temple. So fine was its design and construction, he thought people would come from far and wide to worship there.

Days and weeks passed and yet no one came to the temple. Baffled, the priest hiked down the hill to town to inquire why no one would come to worship there. He was told that many people began the four-mile hike, but about a mile before reaching the temple they were chased away by a huge, vicious python. The villagers were very frightened. It was rumored that the snake had eaten at least four people that year.

Upon hearing this, the priest said he would have a word with the snake, which he did as he headed back home.

"Snake!" he yelled. "You are intimidating the villagers who wish to come to my temple. Why do you do this?"

The enormous reptile slithered from behind a large tree and replied, "The villagers make too much noise. They disturb my sleep. They irritate me no end. In my frustration, I scare them away, so I may have some peace."

"Then I will talk with the people and ask them to be quiet and leave you alone. If they proceed quietly, will you allow them safe passage?" the priest asked.

The snake agreed. So the priest posted a new proclamation announcing his temple with the request that vistors pass silently through the forest on their way there.

When the village folk came to the temple to worship, they were awestruck by its craftsmanship. Its beauty was equal to that of the Taj Mahal. Word spread far and wide and soon people came from faraway lands to worship there.

The priest felt it was time to express his gratitude to the mighty python. He walked down the path to offer his thanks. It wasn't long before he found the snake lying by the side of the path, pulverized, nearly beaten to death.

"Snake! What has happened to you?" the priest asked.

"You told me to let the people pass and I did. In return, one day they came with clubs and repeatedly hit me."

"Snake, I asked you not to strike and bite. I never said you couldn't hiss."

> When you get angry, count to ten, say you're angry, then let it go.

6

Embracing the Shadow

The next time you come to Colorado, plan to visit in the fall, right around the time of the autumnal equinox. At this time of year the leaves of the aspens begin to yellow, setting the mountains ablaze in gold. The elk start their mating season at this time as well, a ritual which is fascinating to watch as the bulls strut around the female cows looking for a date. They emit a peculiar noise from their vocal cords, known in the Rocky Mountain region as "bugling."

Recently a good friend of mine, Darren, called me up announcing plans to move to Colorado. As part of the long-standing spirit of Western hospitality, I offered him a place to stay while he came out to scout jobs and apartments. Darren is quite a handsome guy, with a smile that oscillates between naïveté and danger. He stands six-foot-two and has the kind of body you see on the cover models of men's magazines. Women swoon over him.

It's no secret that Darren has a great many likable qualities. I'm particularly fond of his sense of humor. He's also the best storyteller I know east of the Mississippi. On the day he arrived, the aspens had just starting turning. He took one look at the mountains and told me he was ready to make Colorado his new home. That afternoon, in an attempt to satisfy our cravings to be outdoors, we took a drive up to Rocky Mountain National Park for a hike. Before we even got to the trailhead, we heard scores of bull elk bugling. We climbed up on some rocks for a better view, and, like the other tourists there for the same reason, we became engrossed in this intriguing mating behavior.

It might have been the bull elk prancing around the meadow that became the catalyst for the turn Darren took in the conversation, or it might have just been his mood that particular afternoon, but he cocked his head toward me and said bluntly, "I've started going to therapy."

I turned to look him in the eyes, wondering what he might say next.

"I've come to learn that I have a sexual addiction," he explained. "I have a history of infidelity when I'm in a relationship. I finally admitted to myself I need help. So I began counseling sessions with a therapist back east. He's really good."

The conversation was broken by a disturbance among the herd of twenty elk below. Another bull about 100 yards away was calling to the cows in an attempt to lure them to his harem. One cow got up to check him out. The bull in her group followed. She was quickly redirected back to the meadow, where she eventually sat down.

With peace reestablished among the herd, Darren continued. "As a child all the way through high school, I was really a fat kid. Then one year I got really sick and lost a lot of weight, about forty pounds. When I came back to school I was getting all this attention from the girls. Being a nice guy, I simply tried to be attentive in return. Between hormones, social pressures, and some unresolved family issues, sex became a way to ease my emotions. What started in high school got worse as I got older. In college I had girlfriends, but I could just look at a woman at any party and draw her in. I wasn't devious, although you could certainly call my behavior self-centered."

"So I'm at this wedding a few months ago with my current girlfriend, and during the reception I meet this woman, a friend of the groom, and we start kissing—right in front of my girlfriend. It was then I thought to myself, This is sick! I really need some help."

I motioned to the trail and we got up off the rock and began our hike toward the lake. I was quite impressed with Darren's openness. Here was a friend I had known for ten years. Although our conversations had covered a great many topics over the decade, this was a new level in the depths of personal sharing. I thanked him for revealing this to me.

Darren commented on how hard it was to admit to himself those attributes which are less than flattering. In turn, I commented that he had begun a long but fruitful process of "embracing the shadow," an expression used in Jungian psychology in which we acknowledge the dark side of our persona, the underbelly of the ego. By coming to terms with our insecurities and related behaviors, we embrace, rather than ignore, these aspects. In doing so, we learn to modify our behavior, or, as they say in Eastern cultures, to "domesticate the ego," deflating it to a more manageable, less stress-producing size.

"Sexual addiction is a very common addiction, perhaps too common," Darren explained, "and like other addictions, the fix is short-lived, until the next one comes along.

Before I went to therapy, I thought counseling was for weak sissies. I don't anymore. I think therapy would help a great many people. There are a lot of people like me out there. I know you use a lot of stories in your talks. If you think this will help anyone, you have my permission to use this one too."

The conversation turned once again to the shadow. "My therapist recommended a really good book, called *Out of the Shadows*. I've also started keeping a journal where I write down my moods. It really helps. Now that we've completely covered the topic of infidelity, my therapist wants to explore the topic of abandonment and, of course, anger some more. Layer by layer we're uncovering some really important issues."

We walked in silence for several steps, each of us pondering the challenge that personal growth demands. Darren, who was ahead of me, reached the lake first. He took a seat on a rock at the water's edge. I stood behind the rock, looking up at the sky. Distant thunder broke the silence. Moments later, two ducks flew overhead to circle the body of water, descending slowly for their landing. We talked some more about the growing pains of life and concluded that hard as they are, the end result is worth it. With another clap of thunder, Darren stood up and we decided to head back toward the parking lot.

As we approached the car, the calls of two bull elk reverberated in stereo. Darren smiled at me. "I've decided when I move to Colorado next month, I am not getting involved in a relationship. I've got some more work to do on myself first. And I'm going to try a committed relationship with nature," he said.

All of us have a shadow, a dark side where our less-than-favorable attributes appear. It might be said that this is the shadow of the ego with which we must come to terms, to acknowledge, understand, and reconcile behaviors associated with the dark side. These can range from judgments and prejudices to full-blown addictions. Like an orphaned child, the shadow begs to be embraced. In doing so, we begin to stop the cycle of unhealthy, stress-prone behaviors.

7

Downsize This!

A word that is used synonymously today with stress is change. As a rule, people don't like change. Change tends to disrupt our comfort zones, that area of security created by our thoughts, ideas, perceptions, possessions, even our locale. As the expression says, "The only person who likes change is a wet baby."

As we spin into the twenty-first century, change is not only present, but here with a vengeance. Sociologists tell us that while change has always been a factor in human evolution, the rate of change we are experiencing today is unparalleled in any other time in history. And many people are finding this rate of change quite stressful.

A common reaction to unexpected change is anger. Feelings of anger can manifest in various ways, from impatience to all-out rage. Like an airborne virus, there is much anger in the air today. In my work as a consultant to corporations, conducting stress management seminars, I often come in contact with a great many angry employees, many who will soon be restructured out of their jobs. And because everything connects, the reverberations of changes in the corporate landscape ripple out to reach every community, every family.

It is fair to say that every sensation of anger is the result of an unmet expectation. By and large, most unmet expectations these days deal with job security, or lack thereof. A critical aspect of the American dream is based on job security—the ability to make house payments, finance a child's tuition, or take yearly vacations to exotic getaways. Moreover, the Puritan ethic still dominates the American psyche, where people typically measure their self-worth by the size of their paycheck.

Due to the dynamics of the current corporate landscape, change, in the form of downsizing and right-sizing, is an annoying common occurrence. As such, a lifelong career with one company is increasingly rare, and job security is a thing of the past. While anger is an appropriate response to losing your job, it's important not to get stuck in it. Rather, we must grieve and move on.

Like me, Todd got his aerobic exercise by swimming. I would see him in the pool when I went to do my workout in the early mornings. Our conversations ranged from the temperature of the water to the global economy, and most everything in between. An engineer with a technology company and a young married man with two children, Todd, like most people his age, was seemingly well-situated on the corporate ladder of success.

One day I changed my exercise routine and headed to the pool at mid-morning. As I walked onto the deck the pool was empty, save for one man ready to enter the water in lane five. I walked over and greeted Todd with a handshake.

"On vacation this week?" I asked.

"Yeah, a permanent vacation, you could say," he replied. "I got laid off from work yesterday. Corporate restructuring! Can you believe it?"

"Wow!" I said with a sigh. "Sorry to hear that."

"Me too," said Todd in a huff. "Excuse me, but I have to work off some frustrations." Adjusting his goggles one last time, he dove into the water.

A week later, I saw Todd at the pool again. Standing chest-deep in the water, we talked about his situation once more. He was still angry, but more mellow than he was during our last exchange. He indicated that his severance package was good enough to last a few months and he was taking time to think over his life and spend more time with his children.

It was more than a month later before I saw Todd at the pool, again at mid-morning. This time his eyes were bright with excitement and no trace of resentment was in his voice.

"Howdy Todd. What's up?" I said.

"Things are pretty good. I have started my own consulting company. I'm really enjoying it."

"Hey, that's wonderful!" I replied.

"You know, I never would have thought I could have said this, but losing my job was the best thing that ever could have happened to me. For ten years I felt like I was selling my soul to the company, only to get kicked in the ass. Now I am my own boss. I call the shots. I can truly say I know what it means to feel empowered."

For those people who work through the grieving process of loss, Todd's comments are not uncommon. In times of stress, it is easy to fall into the role of the victim. But to stay there very long is healthy to neither body nor soul. Every unmet expectation is a death and dying process. And every death, big or small, requires grieving.

The personal answer to career changes isn't always self-employment. But the answer is always found within.

> Security is not found in a job, a spouse, or a home. Like the Kingdom of God, security is found within, and when we realize this we can be secure anywhere.

section eight

Holy Moments: Divine Inspirations

A HOLY MOMENT IS A PERSONAL EXPERIENCE where we are embraced by the arms of God. Psychologist Abraham Maslow called these "peak experiences," moments when, through some situation or circumstance, we unexpectedly encounter the divine—however we conceive this to be. With the understanding that we are *always* in the presence of the divine, a holy moment is a conscious recognition of this divine presence, a gentle awakening, of sorts.

Examples of holy moments include mystical dreams, synchronistic events, magical happenings, or a flash of brilliance, to name just a few. Such moments may be extremely brief, but they typically end the same way; each time we kiss the face of God.

Holy moments are mystical and exhilarating. By all accounts, a holy moment is *the* most pleasant human experience. Some people even call it a "spiritual orgasm." Anyone can have a holy moment, and Maslow argued that we should strive to have as many as humanly possible. We may never fully understand them, but this should not dull our appreciation of their mystery.

Distress may grab the headlines each night, but there are two sides of the stress coin: distress and *eustress,* the good kind of stress. If we are honest with our memories, then we know that life's balance sheet is pretty well even with both. A beautiful sunset, a warm, furry puppy, or a reunion with good friends are indeed special events which simply remind us to live in the present moment. Like a pearl in an oyster, holy moments can appear in the ugliest situations, and every stressor is an opportunity for spiritual growth. As Maslow explained, you don't have to climb a mountain to have a peak experience. Holy moments can happen anywhere, at any time.

1

The Day of the Dolphin

On a trip to Florida in 1989 to visit my father, who had retired there, I discovered he had contracted cancer. It was rather unsettling, but he assured me that with chemotherapy it would all be under control. After a few days, he suggested I take the car and drive up to Disney World's Epcot Center, which I had not yet visited. He declined to come along, saying that he had been there so many times that he preferred to sit this one out. Reluctantly, I packed a small suitcase, took the car keys, and headed north toward Orlando.

At the time of my visit, there was a lull in the tourist season. I arrived at the gates to Epcot early and never once encountered an unbearable crowd. Perhaps it was the circumstance of my Florida visit, but Epcot did nothing for me. Where others were amazed and amused, I was bored and discontented—too much plastic, too many mechanical devices, and too many recordings telling visitors to keep "your hands inside the rails." I had planned to spend three days at Disney World, but after the first few hours, all I wanted to do was leave. By day's end, I wound up at the aquarium, watching the fish. A fellow tourist from Nebraska, much more enthralled than I, turned to me and said, "Isn't this place great?" The disappointment on my face spoke volumes. I explained my dismay and my new acquaintance came up with a plan.

"You should go to Sea World," he said. "You can't beat nature, and there is plenty of it there."

I thanked him and considered the possibility as I walked toward my car in the massive parking lot.

Taking his hint, the next morning I woke early and drove over to Sea World. As I waited for the gates to open, I was relieved to see few tourists clamoring to get in. I flashed my ticket to the man at the turnstiles and walked slowly into the grounds, map outstretched, trying to get my bearings on the theme park grounds. I stopped at a small tank and pulled out the day's list of events so I could coordinate my visit. A large part of me still wanted to leave Orlando, while a bigger part of me was concerned about my dad.

I faced the tank and looked up from the schedule for a moment. The deep pool before me was filled with rich, blue water, but there was not a sign of marine life. Every round corner was empty. I returned to the map again, but I was distracted moments later by a noisy splash. There in front of me was a dolphin, nearly out of the water, eye to eye with me, moving its tail back and forth to hold his position. I dropped the map and schedule on the pool edge. Then I smiled.

I don't know why, but suddenly, I felt compelled to put my arms around the dolphin and give it a hug. The embrace seemed to last for minutes, although I know it was less. Then, as if to say good-bye, the dolphin slowly sank back into the water, gave a few clicks, and was gone.

I was pleasantly stunned. I even wondered if I had imagined the whole thing, but my shirt was soaked—this was no hallucination. A lady, another visitor, quickly approached, said hello, and asked me why the dolphin had come to me. I had no idea what to tell her. I was as surprised as she was, perhaps even more so.

I stood at the tank for another twenty minutes hoping to see the dolphin and thank it, but it appeared empty once again. I was left speechless and filled with joy.

> To catch a falling star, you have to stand underneath it.

2

A Fish Called Allison

At the midpoint of every semester in my stress management classes, after I have introduced and the students have practiced a host of coping techniques, I teach something called "confrontation of a stressor." In this exercise, I explain to my students that the concepts of stress management remain only concepts if they are not practiced outside the classroom. To really make them concrete, one must employ these concepts and techniques in times of stress. So I ask students to make a list of their top ten stressors, pick one of the top three—such as a fight with a roommate, issues with parents, or money problems—and come to terms with it, to face it and resolve it. In doing so, I ask that they not come away the victim. Rather, everyone is instructed to walk away the victor, even if there are some cuts and scrapes along the way. I explain that avoidance is the number one coping technique for stress; typically, however, avoidance does nothing to resolve stress and is, rather, the perfect recipe for perpetuating it. Confrontation of a stressor is an exercise in resolving stressors, no matter how big or small.

I give each student two weeks to work on this assignment. They are asked to write about their experience and describe what they learned from it. When I get done explaining the assignment, I get looks from students as if to say, "You've got to be kidding!" On that day, they walk out the classroom door to scores of problems begging to be resolved. Before you give it a try, which I sincerely hope you will, I'd like to tell you a story.

In spring 1991, I had a student named Allison Fisher. Allison was bright, energetic, and beaming with success. A radio and television major, Allison was a graduating senior and looking forward to a promising broadcasting career. In an earlier class assignment in Art Therapy, Allison drew herself as a fish. The picture was quite revealing, even to a novice in art therapy. The fish was an orange color, a goldfish; the color orange signified change. The green plant near the fish symbolized groundedness and stability. If a fish could show confidence, this fish did—an underlying sense of accomplishment through a great many achievements and accolades that Allison shared as she explained her illustration.

Two weeks after I announced this particular assignment, the students filed into class to see a lit candle in the center of the room and the lights dimmed. I invited everyone to sit in a circle around the candle and then asked if they would be willing to share their experiences with confronting their stressors. In a typical fashion, I explained that we are all teachers and we can learn from each other. I asked that no one pass judgment if a particular student's choice in dealing with a stressor differed from their own. They all agreed.

First I shared my experience. Then I asked for a volunteer. Allison spoke next.

"My stressor is breast cancer, it runs in my family," she explained. "My mother has had it, my aunt, and my grandmother too. For a great many years, I have been scared of breast cancer, even though I know that I, too, am at risk. So upon hearing this assignment, I decided it was time to go for a mammogram. I was extremely nervous, but, last week I made an appointment with my physician."

The class was silent, all eyes fixed on Allison. With an air of confidence, she concluded her story with a nervous smile. "The test was negative. What did I learn from this experience? I learned that by running away from my fear I was really running toward it. Making us do this assignment was hard, but I now know that I can face anything," she said. Little did we know how prophetic these words would be for her.

One by one, each student shared his or her story. One student coming to terms with a promiscuous past took an AIDS test. Another student renewed her relationship with her estranged father. Another student quit her job to focus on schoolwork. Yet another confided about a recent abortion. By the end of the hour, the students had formed a powerful support group. Much healing took place that afternoon.

Five years later, I was visiting a colleague who happened to mention a friend of hers who had survived breast cancer. "A classic case of heredity," Karen said. "Her grandmother, her mother, and now her." Then came more bad news. Her friend, who was now living in Los Angeles and working in a job in broadcast media, had been diagnosed with breast cancer once again.

"Are you speaking of Allison?" I inquired.

"Why, yes, do you know her?" Karen said.

"Yes, she was a student of mine," I said, shocked and saddened at the news. I thought back to the illustration of the goldfish and something told me it was going to be all right.

Later that summer, I found myself in L.A. on a book tour and arranged to meet Allison for lunch. We shared snippets of our lives after each of us left The American University.

It was Allison who brought up the subject of cancer. She shared with me her healing journey, her dissatisfaction with some of her physicians, her disdain for the health care system ("a sick care system," she called it), and her introduction to various forms of complementary medicine—herbs, t'ai chi, homeopathy, and acupuncture.

The focus of the conversation shifted to an award she had won as a promising black leader in broadcast journalism. Allison was beaming. "I want to be involved with quality programming on television. There is so much junk out there," she explained, glowing with vitality. I thought to myself, if there is anyone who can do it, it's Allison. I later learned that Allison played no small part in social activism, assuming the role of a Big Sister, and volunteered countless hours of community service to help the city's underserved population.

On a recent trip to L.A., for my last book signing, I saw Allison again. She had unsettling news. The cancer was back, this time in her lungs. She was going to take time off from her graduate studies and focus all her energies on healing.

That night, as I gave my last book presentation, I

thought about the nature of healing and wholeness. As I have taught my students, healing is the integration, balance, and harmony of mind, body, spirit, and emotions. Healing differs from curing in that it's not simply about removing symptoms of disease and illness. Healing is coming to a sense of peace about who we are and why we are here, no matter the course of our illness. Allison is at that place of peace. In the words of Carl Jung, we come into the world to bring light into the darkness, and Allison has done just that!

> When you were born, you cried and your family rejoiced. Live your life so that when you die, you rejoice and your family cries.

P.S. Allison Fisher crossed the threshold of heaven on March 9, 1998.

3

Tell Me About Your Saints!

I am convinced that there are many saints walking among us. More often than not, they are unrecognized by the general public and definitely not canonized by any church. These people are the real unsung heroes of humanity, and it is only with hindsight that we may ever know their true identity, for they don't seek the public eye and their names are never mentioned in the headline news. But they are the teachers of compassion in action.

It is not uncommon in the course of a workshop for people to ask me why such chaos has entered their lives—illness, the death of a loved one, bankruptcy. So many of us face such difficult circumstances. Is it fate? Maybe karma? Who knows? We many never understand why catastrophic events befall us. Rather than shake our fists at the sky, it might be best to take a deep breath and count our blessings. Perhaps instead of seeing ourselves as victims we should look upon ourselves as teachers. Indeed, it is a courageous soul who braves the harsh emotional elements of Planet Earth, for the responsibility of daily life is a heavy load. This is a story I have shared to comfort those who seek to remove the yoke of victimhood.

Several years ago, I had an enlightening conversation with an acquaintance over a pita sandwich on this very topic. Originally from Asia, Ranjan was in the United States for graduate studies. It was a common interest in tennis that brought us together, but being rather new to the Western world with an insatiable appetite for Western culture, Ranjan soon turned the conversation to other topics.

On this day, after swallowing a bite of his sandwich, he took a sip of iced tea and said, "Tell me about your saints."

After mentally switching gears, I looked up with a smile and replied, "If you knew my behavior as a child, you'd realize I am the last person to answer this question." Not satisfied with my reply, he repeated his question, "Tell me about your saints."

Trying to sound as intelligent as I could with what I felt was an inadequate background in matters of theology, yet keeping my tongue partially in my cheek, I proceeded to explain the nature of sainthood in the Catholic Church.

"Well, as I understand it, a saint's life begins like anyone else's, really. But within a few years, perhaps a few decades, things go downhill. Usually there is some transformational life crisis they experience, but just when all seems lost, there is some divine intervention, an epiphany, and this individual's life is transformed to do good deeds for humanity.

"Oh," I added, "there is one more thing. They have to perform a few miracles before they die. But it doesn't end there. To qualify as a real saint, anyone up for nomination has to do a miracle or two after they die as well, otherwise, they are out of contention.

"The whole process is quite complicated. It's kind of like getting nominated for an Academy Award, and sometimes just as political," I concluded with a faint smile.

I paused, and glanced up at my friend to observe his reaction.

He looked attentive and intrigued. "I see," he said.

After a few more bites on our sandwiches, with an air of curiosity, I started up the conversation again. Naively I asked, "Are there saints in your culture?"

"Yes," he replied, "but not quite as you have described."

What he said next brought comfort to my mind, and continues to do so each time I reflect on it. His words made more clear an understanding of the mysteries of life—those moments of mayhem or misfortune may be intended for a higher purpose, to help others. While the burden is indeed heavy, there is no room for victimhood.

"In our culture," he continued, "we believe each person lives many lives. When one reaches a point where one has balanced all his or her karma, they come to a place we call nirvana, what you might call heaven. Yet there are those souls who, given the chance to move to a higher level of consciousness, hesitate. For as great as the pleasures this new journey holds, a few souls look back with regret because the peace of heaven is a shallow victory when not shared by those they loved on earth. So, in an effort to help elevate the souls of their loved ones, they brave the dense earthly existence once more. In most every case they take on a hardship, a disease, some catastrophe or burden for the sole purpose of providing an opportunity for love to manifest from the hearts of those they touch. These are the ones we call saints."

Each burden we carry is an opportunity for spiritual growth, not only for ourselves but for those with whom we come in contact as well. Carry your burden gracefully. Likewise, be mindful of those you walk past or meet, for there are saints among us everywhere.

4

Cell Memory and Body Wisdom

After presenting a seminar to a group of educators in Des Moines, Iowa, I was approached by a young woman who introduced herself as Sheila. She was quite moved by something I had said. In my talk I had explained that every cell pulsates with energy that is directly connected to our emotions through substances called neuropeptides.

Citing the work of my colleague Candace Pert, who is credited with discovering this mind-body link, I then went on to discuss the concept of cell memory and body wisdom, particularly new discoveries with organ transplant recipients. Apparently not only cell tissue is exchanged during an organ transplant. Part of the donor's human spirit, contained in each cell, goes along for the ride (to learn more about this, read *The Heart's Code* by Paul Pearsall or *A Change of Heart* by Claire Sylvia). I cited some remarkable examples of cell consciousness, and it was this that inspired Shelia to share her story with me.

A nurse for the Des Moines County School District, Sheila was moved by an article she saw in the paper one day about bone marrow transplants. Feeling blessed by her physical health, Sheila heard a calling to investigate what this was all about. So, in April 1997, she signed up for a test to see if she was eligible to make a donation—the gift of renewed life.

For Sheila, making a donation was more than an altruistic act. In her heart, she felt a drive to help someone else in his or her healing process. She explained to me that although she had been through the typical experiences that test our patience, she was now on an even keel. She was happy and felt the need to share it. At age twenty-five, it wasn't curiosity that lured Sheila to be tested for donating bone marrow, it was compassion.

"They do a blood test to see if there is a possible match through tissue type. As I was tested, I was told that there is a one in two million chance of having a match. As I walked to my car, I kind of forgot about it. But then a week later, I received a phone call to confirm the test—there was a match. I was so excited."

The match was an eight-year-old girl with leukemia. Sheila was scheduled for a bone marrow extraction and then waited to hear about the results. "When you donate bone marrow, you're not allowed direct personal contact with the recipient for a whole year. I sent her cards and a cute little teddy bear. But I felt a bond with this little girl like you wouldn't believe. It went far beyond thinking about her and corresponding with her. I could feel myself as a part of her, and perhaps equally strange, I could feel her in me."

Sheila described this bond as being so strong that she could practically feel her bone marrow cells in the little girl's body. Things changed dramatically on July 29 that year, for on this day, Sheila learned that Laurie Minor, the eight-year-old girl whom Sheila had bonded with in spirit and body cells, had died.

"It was all so devastating. Never once did I think that it wouldn't work," Sheila explained. But something happened that Sheila finds difficult to put into words. As she described it, "Just as I became a part of her, she became a part of me. It's as if I can now feel her presence. I know she's with me."

Within a few months, the girl's mother contacted her. "I think our meeting was healing for all of us. I saw some photographs and videotapes of Laurie. Let me tell you, this kid was full of life. She may not be here on earth, but her vitality is still very present," Sheila said.

Sheila's life has been changed from the experience. When not performing her role as a school nurse, she is actively involved in fund-raising activities, primarily for bone marrow transplants.

"Through Laurie's parents, I met Dan Burl, the executive director of STRIDE, an organization that puts on charity events for leukemia patients. Dan Burl, it turns out, ran a marathon to raise money for Laurie's medical expenses. Next year I am going to run a marathon in Disney World to raise money," Sheila explained. "I have over $2,000 so far and a new purpose in my life." And the spirit of Laurie Minor lives on.

> Life is a balance of giving and receiving. There is pleasure and pain in both. The physiology and spirituality of stress, both good and bad, reside in every cell. As the advances in technology increase our ability to prolong life, so too, do the mysteries

of life unfold. Gifts of the heart need not be big, only sincere, in order to make a big difference in the world.

5

A Cosmic Joke

Just as stress and spirituality are partners in the dance of life, so too are fate and free will. But if there is an overriding game plan to our lives, and I believe there is, then certain forces will prevail to right us on our track should we stray too far from the divine game plan. Synchronistic moments are more than an acknowledgment and appreciation of our divine connectedness. Quite possibly, they are signs of the cosmic correction factor when free will has taken a turn that is not in our best interest.

Katy is a dear friend of mine. We attended college together at the University of Maine. Fifteen years later, I was living in Washington, D.C. She had just changed jobs in Boston, and she had some time off before she started at a new advertising firm. She called one evening to chit-chat and get caught up on things, as we typically did once or twice a year. This phone call was different, though. She called to tell me she was dating a guy named Stanley and that he had just proposed to her; she was now engaged. Although excited for her, something was amiss in her voice. I could tell she was aware of it too.

Later in the conversation she indicated that there was something a little off in the relationship with Stanley, but she couldn't quite put her finger on it. "No relationship is perfect," I commented. As the conversation continued, Katy mentioned that Stanley had left for Europe on business and would be gone two weeks. It had been over five years since Katy and I had visited, so I invited her down to the nation's capital for the weekend, to get away and gain perspective on things. She agreed.

Friday night we fixed dinner and talked for hours. The plan was to go sightseeing on Saturday. Although I had the best intentions to be a good tour guide, I also had exams to grade over the weekend. So, excusing myself for a few hours, I dropped Katy off at the nearest Metro stop, gave her complete instructions on D.C.'s superb subway rail system, and off she went to explore the Smithsonian.

In D.C., clocks are set in a time warp. Everyone is late. On that day, so was I. Consequently, I missed our appointed rendezvous at Metro Center by almost an hour. I ran up to Katy at the platform to apologize, but there was no forgiveness on her face. She was livid! As I tried to explain, she waved her hands. Within seconds I was to learn that I wasn't the focus of her anger. What she proceeded to tell me was beyond belief. More accurately, it was divine intervention through the grace of synchronicity. The morning at the Metro stop was not merely the chance coupling of two random events. But first, let me set the stage.

Each Metro train has about ten cars, with two doors on each side. Trains come and go every few minutes, with hundreds of people entering and exiting the subway cars at each stop. To a visitor, it looks like mass confusion. To

D.C. residents, it's just organized chaos. The chances of what was to happen that morning at the platform, before I appeared, are a zillion to one. Katy was waiting patiently for a train to arrive and take her to the Smithsonian. Lights flashed on the platform indicating a train was approaching. The Metro pulled up and came to a stop. The train doors opened, directly in front of Katy, and out stepped Stanley, holding hands with another woman. Katy was aghast! She just stared at him in disbelief. Their eyes met and locked. In less than a nanosecond, Stanley yelled out to Katy, "What are *you* doing here?" Then, as if the imposition was too much to handle, he turned and quickly walked away, arm in arm with the woman.

Once Katy calmed down, I said, "Wow! I think God is trying to tell you something here."

We made our exit aboveground and headed to the Pavilion for lunch. It didn't take long for her to realize the meaning of the coincidence. Later, over a cup of coffee, she confided that intuitively she felt he was seeing other women, but a part of her (ego, perhaps?) just wasn't ready to admit it—until now. In the course of a few hours, grief yielded to humor, as Katy was able to smile at the cosmic joke played on her.

> There are no random events in the universe. A coincidence is God's way of remaining anonymous.

6

For Pete's Sake

Of all the stories in my book *Stand Like Mountain, Flow Like Water,* one seems to bring up more questions than the rest. It's the story of Peter, the little boy with bone cancer. People often ask me how he is. Until a few months ago, I could only answer, "I don't know." But as fate would have it, I ran into Pete once again. Here is his story and, as Paul Harvey says, "the rest of the story."

I met Peter Knutgen on a plane ride from Denver to Los Angeles. Typically I use time in the air to recharge my personal energy, so I don't engage too often in conversations with fellow passengers. This trip was different. I struck up a conversation with Peter because for the entire trip, his foot rested on my lap. Peter had the window seat (mine, actually), I had the aisle, and his mother sat in between us. The weight of his leg suggested a pretty heavy cast somewhere between his seat and mine.

Peter, I learned, was ten years old, heading out on a trip to Disneyland.

"So," I began the conversation, "Tell me about your leg."

"Well" said Peter, "I was diagnosed with bone cancer a few months ago. I had an operation which is why my leg is in a cast. It's OK! They thought they might have to amputate, but it turns out my leg's fine," Peter explained.

"I was rather upset, as you can imagine," he continued, "but I realized something soon after I learned I had cancer."

"Oh yeah," I said, "what's that?"

"Well, I remembered seeing this TV show. Every kid who has cancer gets to make a wish. You know what my wish was?" he inquired with an optimistic smile.

"No, what was it?" I asked.

"Well I always wanted to swim with dolphins, and you know what? I did! I made my wish and it came true. Last month I swam with some dolphins in Florida."

I sat in my seat, 35,000 feet above the earth, smiling at a little boy with blond hair and a great big smile, thinking to myself, this kid has so much optimism, he doesn't need a plane to get to L.A. Hearing Peter's story, I thought, with his level of optimism, I'll bet there isn't a cancer cell left in his body.

Peter's mom, Bonnie, jumped into the conversation. "Tell the man about what you're doing now, Peter."

"I've become a spokesperson for the Make-a-Wish Foundation," Peter said with a smile. "I go around and give motivational talks to kids like me who have cancer."

Here's a kid, I thought, who has definitely made lemonade from lemons.

The conversation jumped around various topics before the plane landed, and soon we were at the baggage claim area before we parted ways.

Before I tell "the rest of the story," a little background information is needed. For the past two decades, people unknown to me have approached me and asked me for my autograph. As it turns out, they don't want my autograph, they want that of the person they think I look like. Since his "JT" album came out in 1975, I have been mistaken for singer James Taylor at least two to three times a week—for over twenty years! I have to admit, there is a striking similarity in our facial features, even mannerisms and expressions (despite the fact that he is five inches taller than I). I once met his brother, Livingston Taylor, and the first thing he said to me was, "God, you look just like my brother."

This particular summer, James Taylor was coming to do a benefit concert for the NPR program "E-Town." I decided to buy a ticket. I thought that if I had the chance to meet him, shake his hand, and get a photo, perhaps I could "break the spell," so to speak.

That night at dinner in a downtown restaurant I got stared at a lot. Three times I was asked, "Are you James Taylor?" The concert wasn't for another two hours and I knew it was going to be a long night. I took my seat inside the theater and waited for the show to start.

After the first set, there was a twenty-minute intermission. I decided to head down to the stage and see if I could meet my "double." Stage hands just gave me double-takes. People walked by and pointed. I turned my back to the audience and waited.

As I stood there I saw, from the corner of my eye, a teenager approach me.

"Hey," he said, "Are you . . ." (All I could think of was, please kid, don't ask me that question.)

Then came the rest of the question: "Brian Luke Seaward?"

I was stunned. Somebody actually knew *me*—a first at any concert. Who was this person?

"Yes," I answered. "Who are you?"

"I'm Peter Knutgen," he said with a huge smile. "The guy with two great legs."

It had been over five years since I had met Peter. Boy, had he grown! He was nearly six feet tall. I barely recognized him. I reached to shake his adult-size hand and then proceeded to give him a hug. It was a special reunion.

"So Peter," I said, "how the heck are you?"

Tapping on his left leg, he answered, "Good as new."

I had no doubts. I gave him another big hug and wished him well, knowing quite well he really didn't need it.

A few weeks later I got a letter from him. It read,

> Dear Dr. Seaward,
>
> It was so nice to see you again at the James Taylor concert. I was happy to see that you have been living well. I hope this letter finds you in the same condition as when our paths have crossed on the two previous occasions. You seem like a very upbeat, positive person, and it has been very pleasant spending time with you.
>
> Lately I have been doing very well and I have simply been having a blast in life.
>
> Hope to see you again soon.
>
> Sincerely,
> *Peter*

Follow Peter's lead and seize the day, no matter your troubles.

7

The Man Who Wouldn't Die

How do you know when your life-mission is complete? In the words of Richard Bach, author of the book *Illusions,* if you're still alive it means there is work remaining to be finished. Such is the case of Seaborn "Beck" Weathers.

By now most everyone has heard of the ill-fated event on Mt. Everest in summer 1996, when nine climbers died. Perhaps the most remarkable point of this story is about one of the climbers, who was left for dead—twice—but actually lived.

Beck Weathers is a physician from Dallas, Texas. His ascent toward the top of Everest that summer was his first, and like many others in his party, there was the usual apprehension. On that fateful day, when his team of climbers was set to reach the summit, a ferocious storm blew in, leaving a handful in his party stranded for hours in subfreezing temperatures as night set in. Extremely tired, cold, fighting for oxygen, and practically blinded from the inhospitable weather, Beck's condition, which, like the weather, was poor at the start of the day, only got worse that evening. In an attempt to warm his right hand

and place it in his jacket, he took off his mittens, only to watch the wind carry them off the mountain. Left unshielded, his hands were to become casualties of the harshest of elements.

One team member from the fractured group braved the ferocious elements to find the camp and return with help. When a group of rescuers returned hours later, Beck Weathers was found lying in a snowbank, severely frostbitten and presumed dead. Since there was no way to bring his body back, he was left there, as many corpses are. Early next morning, however, Beck Weathers woke from what teammate Jon Krakauer, author of the account of that expedition, *Into Thin Air,* described as a "hypothermic coma." As if guided by unseen forces, Beck made his way back to camp, missing a precipice that would surely have ended his life had he fallen from it. His return to camp amazed everyone, but those who saw him knew his time left on earth was indeed very short.

In an essay for the National Geographic book, *Everest: Mountain Without Mercy,* Beck wrote of his first of two episodes at the edge of death, "Sometime the next afternoon, I found myself alone on the ice. I was not terribly uncomfortable, and I was convinced I was dreaming. The hardest part was coming to grips with the fact that my situation was real and serious. I rolled over and looked at my hand, which appeared like an unnatural, plastic twisted gray thing attached to the end of my arm—not at all the hand I knew. I banged it on the ice, and it made a hollow sound, a sickening thunk."

With his right hand, forearm, and nose completely frostbitten, he lay in his sleeping bag hovering on the verge of death. Those in camp who could descend to the lower camp did. Assuming he was too weak to follow, Beck was once again left to die on the mountain. Hours later, however, he shuffled into the lower-elevation camp, once again defying the odds and apparently the grip of death as well.

"I had a heck of a lot to live for and wasn't going down easy," said Beck. My family [an image in his mind], standing there before me became an incredible driving force.... When a middle-aged guy like me can survive that, it gives truth to the possibility that this kind of strength resides in each of us."

At this point he got help from others, one of whom was David Breashears, a world-renowned climber from a different party, which had set out at the same time to make an IMAX film of their expedition to the top of Everest. In a slide presentation made to a Boulder audience a year later, Breashears described his personal experience with this most remarkable man.

"Beck Weathers has an incredible sense of humor, and I am convinced this is what got him through his ordeal. We were tied together with a rope walking down, and he turns to me and says, 'You know, I told my wife, Peach, that this trip was going to cost me an arm and a leg. Little did I know!' And then later he breaks into a version of the song 'Chain Gang.' I wanted to say, 'Beck, how can you be making jokes about something like this? Stop this.' But Beck told me he had to, it was the only way to survive such a harrowing ordeal."

And that he did.

> We can only speculate as to why some die while others live in a single moment of tragedy. If we are still alive, then our work here on earth, whatever that might be, is still to be completed.

8

Stand Like Mountain, Move Like Water

After giving a presentation on the topic of stress and human spirituality at a conference in summer 1996, I was approached by a man who introduced himself as a singer/songwriter who wrote songs giving a similar message. Sticking his hand out to shake mine, he thanked me for my talk, asked me for a business card, and, waving a quick good-bye, said he would be in touch. I meet several hundred wonderful people this way each year. I have come to appreciate that even if our only encounter begins and ends with a handshake, hug, or smile, it is a special one. After several more conferences and workshops that summer, the musician's handshake accompanied by his leprechaun smile faded from memory.

But I did hear from him again, later that summer. One day, walking back from my mailbox, my curiosity was piqued by a package from TuneTown Records. Inside were two CDs from Greg Tamblyn. I recognized the photogenic smile on the album cover. I walked over to the CD player and put the first one in, then smiled, laughed, and pondered for the next fifty minutes of musical interludes and witty lyrics. The second CD had the same effect. Greg's promotional materials revealed that he spent several years as a singer/songwriter in Nashville, followed by a calling to tour on his own. His concert schedule typically includes Unity Churches, mind-body medicine conferences, and exotic beach resorts. In the accompanying letter Greg wrote, "You talk about the topics I sing about. We should write a song together sometime."

About a year later, Greg and I sat in my living room discussing the possibilities of collaborating on a song. I told him of my new project, *Stand Like Mountain, Move Like Water,* a book on the topic of stress and human spirituality (the title was slightly changed at press time). I recall mentioning to him that although the title was drawn from a Chinese proverb, in my mind I could definitely hear someone like Mary Chapin Carpenter singing a song with the same title, perhaps with a folk or country flair to it. With an elfish smile, Greg said, "Yeah, and she's the only one who could pull it off, too!"

In the course of the afternoon we discussed several concepts in the soon-to-be published book. Briefly skimming the manuscript, Greg said emphatically, "I love the title."

Over a glass of iced tea, I commented that I saw two possibilities for a song. The first was a story of a person who triumphs over stress. The second was a song about the theme of the book: stress provides the opportunity for spiritual growth. I recall making a comment that the song should have a special essence, underscoring the divine nature of the human condition. Greg agreed. At the end of the day, he waved good-bye with a reassuring nod that a song was, indeed, in the works.

There are many lessons I have learned on the nature of stress and human spirituality, but one of the most profound is the idea that although space and time seem to separate things, all things connect. Chief Seattle said it, Einstein said it, and Jung said it, to name a few. Something undetected by the five senses, immeasurable by Western science yet obvious to the intuitive mind, something mystical (the poets say it's love), unites everything together. In the fast-paced lifestyles we live, our myopia often blinds us to this connection. In fact, our rushed and hectic demeanor tends to reinforce the illusion of separation. But every once in a while, we are jolted into remembering.

That's what happened to me and Greg. Months later, in what can only be described as a divine moment of synchronicity, Greg began to write the lyrics to "our" song based on a story he read in the *Kansas City Star,* about a Chinese woman who had been imprisoned for nearly seven years, falsely accused of being a spy for the British government. The woman's name was Nien Cheng, and she wrote a book describing her ordeal, *Life and Death in Shanghai*. Nien is a friend of mine and I shared her story in the first chapter of *Stand Like Mountain.* While Greg was composing the song, I hit the road on a seven-month book tour. During that time, I pretty much forgot about the song project.

I arrived home one day in October to find a package from Greg in the mail. I placed my suitcase by the hall closet, walked over to the stereo, and placed the demo tape in the tape deck. My eyes welled up with tears of joy as I listened. Let me tell you, Mary Chapin Carpenter's got nothing over Greg Tamblyn (and co-songwriter Richard Helm). The CD, *Art from the Heart,* recorded in Nashville, arrived in the mail around the Christmas holidays. However, it wasn't until March 1998 that the magic of the song was truly revealed.

"Greg, I sent a copy of the CD to Nien Cheng. She was very moved," I said in a late-night phone call to Kansas City.

"You mean you *know* her?" Greg asked.

"Sure, she's a friend of mine. Didn't I mention to you that I wrote about her in the book?" I replied.

"I had absolutely no idea, I don't think you even told me."

"You mean you wrote this song about her not knowing her story was in the book? I cannot believe it," I said in astonishment.

"Amazing! Simply amazing," Greg replied in disbelief.

We both laughed, understanding at last just how divinely inspired our collaboration really was.

Stand Like Mountain, Move Like Water

(Greg Tamblyn, Richard Helm, and
Brian Luke Seaward, TuneTown Records)

At the foot of a mountain, in a bamboo café
Sat an old Asian lady with eyes full of grace
I felt myself drawn to her calm quiet way
And as her story started to flow, I was carried away

She told of a night when soldiers appeared
And chained her in darkness for seven long years
There's a wall in her country a thousand miles long
And they wrapped it around her for thinking all wrong

Chorus:

Stand like mountain, move like water
Earth and heaven have this to offer
Strength will flow from life with honor
Stand like mountain, move like water

She knew in her heart that she committed no crime
And a story to tell is what kept her alive
In a cell with no windows she nurtured the seed
That one day light would shine in and people would see

I thought how her life was so different from mine
And the insight that came has remained in my mind
Here is a woman who knows who she is
Through good times and bad, she's the same, the way that she lives

At the foot of a mountain in a bamboo café
We bowed to each other and I made my way
And I carry with me like the seeds on the wind
Her spirit and her story to tell, and so it begins

Perhaps there is no such thing as a coincidence, a purely random occurrence of two events. I believe holy moments are the connection points in the web of life. They lend balance to what some might call the unholy moments of life's tensions and frustrations. An ancient proverb states, "God is the maestro, and we are divine instruments." May we honor the connection so that when we meet, we make beautiful music together.

9

Heaven and Hell

In the past fifteen years, I have read many accounts of near-death experiences, but recently, in the course of three days, I met two people who told me their heading-toward-the light adventures. Ironically, both had very similar stories.

"Do you believe in guardian angels?" I was asked point-blank by Eric, a middle-aged banking executive.

Before I could give an answer, Eric proceeded to tell me why he did. I was to learn there was no doubt in his mind whatsoever!

"I believe we each have a guide who watches over us. I know I do." As he said this, he threw his leg up on the table, rolled up his pant leg, and showed me a scar the size of a half-dollar, four inches below his knee. "Ten years ago, I was electrocuted." Pointing to the scar he explained, "That's where it exited. I was dead for over a half an hour—no heart rate, no blood pressure—well beyond brain damage time. The paramedics explained to me later that the hospital was just too far away. I was on my way to the morgue. Imagine their surprise when I came to!"

He stopped to organize his thoughts. For a subject as ineffable as this, he was determined to be as articulate as he could. "It's true what they say about the light. It's hard to describe. It's like nothing here on earth. The only way to describe it is wonderful. The physician who treated me tried to explain this as some biochemical process going on in my dying brain, but he couldn't explain what else I saw. He also couldn't explain why my internal organs weren't fried. People who are electrocuted look like they have been microwaved inside. The kidneys, liver, and heart get cooked like burnt toast, but not mine!"

Again, Eric paused to formulate his thoughts. "I saw my brother, who had died two years previously. I saw this entity which I can only guess was my guardian angel. It might have been God, but I personally don't think we have the mind to comprehend what God really is. I saw my whole life reviewed before my very eyes. Let me tell you this; it wasn't pretty. I think the hell they talk about is the sensation of intense pain you experience when you realize all the hurt you have inflicted on other people. Heaven is the rush of love you feel afterward, as you move closer to the light."

Michael's story was nearly identical. He and a neighbor were clearing some dead branches in his mother's backyard when his chainsaw touched a high-voltage wire and Boom! His neighbor was airborne and knocked unconscious. At that same moment, over two thousand houses in the community lost power. Michael took a trip to the next dimension.

"It is so hard to describe, but the most real experience I have ever had. I was moving at warp speed, you know, like the *U.S.S. Enterprise* on *Star Trek*. I saw hundreds of faces, not really human faces, more like spiritual entities. Then there was the light."

From her living room window, Michael's mother and sister saw the whole thing. Each gasped in horror. Both women saw Michael's body simply vanish, as if it vaporized. His body seemed to have disappeared, but all the while his soul migrated toward a bright, loving light for a brief but memorable visit.

When he "reappeared" moments later, he was standing, fully conscious. The soles of both boots were completely blown off his feet. A utility crew arrived shortly thereafter and they couldn't believe Michael was alive, uninjured, and had sustained no internal damage!

"Before this event, I knew God was around, but I always thought I was in charge. I'm no longer afraid to ask for help. I know there is a protective force in my life," he said.

"Now, let me tell you something. Whatever happened opened something up in my mind. Since that day, my values have changed. I appreciate everything. I don't take anything for granted anymore. I know I am here to experience and share unconditional love, like the kind that I experienced on the other side. In truth, that's what we're all here for, most of us just don't know it. And I might add, the world could use a lot of love right now.

"You know," Mike concluded, "you don't have to experience death to know heaven or hell. They're both right here on earth. Each moment we make a choice in what direction we move toward. I've already made my decision."

The difference between heaven and hell, for some, is a matter of perception. The same can be said about stress. Stress is a perception: where we chose to place our attention, and how we choose to use our intention. To some extent, both heaven and hell are here on earth. Where do you place your attention and intention?

10

To Do the Work of Angels

The fear of death is considered by many folks to be the worst fear of all. Second to love, the topic of death has made for the most profound subject matter in classic plays, operas, poems, songs, and books. For many of us, this is as close as we want to get to death. Simply put, death is much too stressful to face head-on, whether it's our own mortality or that of someone close to us. Avoidance is a common coping technique, albeit an ineffective one. In truth, death cannot be avoided.

American culture has a way of shielding the process of dying from our collective consciousness. As if the consequences might prove to be too painful, the topic of death and dying, not to mention exposure to it, are often sanitized to become more palatable. It is quite possible today to go through life and never see a dying loved one or a deceased relative, while in other cultures, and even in this country a century ago, to be in the presence of a dying person was not an uncommon occurrence.

The work of people like Elizabeth Kübler-Ross and Steven Levine have brought dignity to the topic of death and dying, and have helped minimize the element of fear involved with this stressful event. In Kübler-Ross' words, "No one should ever have to die alone." The hospice movement, which she helped pioneer several decades ago, has been remarkable in its efforts to maintain the dignity of chronically ill and dying patients. My first exposure to the mission of hospice work came in the last few days as my aunt was dying of stomach cancer. It was then I knew, unequivocally, that no one should ever die alone. A year later I was to face death again, this time with more direct contact and closer heart-strings. Although I was not afraid of death, in hindsight I realized that this time, I had a special role to play.

My father was a project engineer for a large aerospace company. In 1978 he was transferred to Florida, where he worked for several years before he retired to play endless games of golf and take countless deep-sea fishing trips. In spring 1993, I was making a career transition from Washington, D.C. to Boulder, Colorado. It was at this time, a year after his sister's death from cancer, that I learned that, he too, had been diagnosed with cancer—again. "Not to worry," he assured me. "It's nothing. It will be gone in no time." I took his comment at face value. I'm sure there was an element of denial on my part, and perhaps his as well.

By the end of August I had a strong premonition that all was not well, despite his assurances to the contrary. So I canceled several speaking engagements and quickly made plans to visit him at the end of September. Three days before my scheduled departure, I received a phone call from my sister, who lives nearby, telling me that indeed, Dad was deathly ill. "Get here as soon as you can.

He's on his last leg and asking for you," she cried.

Greeted at the airport by his wife, I was quickly briefed on my father's condition. He had over sixteen tumors, and his condition was well beyond the effective range of chemotherapy and radiation treatment. He had a week at the most, she explained, perhaps only a few days. Through her tears, she tried to warn me about how bad he looked. When I walked into his bedroom, the man I knew as my childhood hero was nothing more than a frail, emaciated skeleton. It was quite shocking and, despite his wife's warning, I was still caught off-guard. Dad offered a weak smile, raised his arm to shake hands, and then closed his eyes in fatigue.

That first night, lying in bed, I reflected on the man I knew as my father. Baseball was his passion. He had even been recruited by the Red Sox before WWII, but had been drafted into the Navy instead. He valued a good education (he was a Yale graduate), yet advocated travel as life's "real school." He secretly admired Vince Lombardi and always rooted for the Green Bay Packers. I remembered his taste for fine restaurants, excellent wine (perhaps too much wine), the stock market, and Ian Fleming novels. As an aircraft engineer, he somehow made planes fly, but his work with the government never allowed him to talk about his job.

He married young. His first wife, a nurse, caught tuberculosis and died. He never talked about her. At the age of twenty-three, he contracted tuberculosis himself and nearly died as well. Three years later, he married my mother. She died in 1981. He was stoic, yet had a good sense of humor. Being myself more of a right-brain person, in contrast to his left-brain personality, I never really knew what he thought of my work and interest in matters of stress and human spirituality—that is, until this visit. That night, as he lay in the next room, I stared at the ceiling for many hours, knowing a chapter was closing in his life and mine.

During my short visit, there was plenty of time to talk, joke around, smile, and reminisce. On what was scheduled to be my last day, my father took a serious turn for the worse. My sister and stepmother were absent (in their grief, they explained, they could just not be with him), so I sat alone by his side, holding his hand, whispering loving words of kindness and veiled glimpses into his future. Early that morning a knock at the door informed me the hospice nurse arrived for what was to be her final visit. Because of a hectic schedule she couldn't stay long, she explained, as she made her way to her next appointment. I sat in silence and prayed. As my father's breaths grew extremely shallow drawing down to his final inspiration, I held his hand tightly and offered my love, and congratulations on his transition.

I would like to say the room grew bright at his passing, but if it did, I didn't notice. There was certainly an air of calmness and a feeling of what I could only call "grace." Within moments of his passing, I was moved to open the windows, perhaps as a symbolic gesture of his soul's freedom. Then I left the room to tell his wife that my dad had died, and I offered her a warm embrace.

> There is nothing to fear in death. In the words of Elizabeth Kübler-Ross, "I want to assure you that it is a blessing to sit at the bedside of a dying patient. What you learn from dying patients you

can pass on to your children and to your neighbors, and maybe our world would become a paradise again. I believe the time to start is now."

11

From Hope to Faith in Thirty Years

As a consultant for a midwestern hospital, I was invited to spend a weekend in Arizona to plan a retreat for the hospital's board of directors. The theme of the retreat was integrating complementary medicine (the new name for alternative medicine) into the existing practice of Western medicine. Rather than lodge in a hotel, we were invited to stay as guests of one of the retreat planning committee members. Hotels being generally rather stuffy, we readily agreed. The drive from Phoenix to Sedona was about two and a half hours. When we arrived at the house, we found a note on the door and a key under the mat. Carolyn, our host, worked at an area hospital and would arrive back in a few hours. So we began to make ourselves at home.

Upon entering her house, I could not help but notice a rather large montage of photographs on the wall heading from the living room down the hall to the bedrooms. The montage depicted the family history of Carolyn, her husband, and their children, from black and white photos of the couple's wedding to color photographs of her two children. Her son, I could tell, was about twenty-five years old, had blond hair and blue eyes, was in the armed services, and had recently married—in a full military wedding. Her daughter, dark-haired and dark-eyed, seemed a year or two older and, as far as I could tell, wasn't married.

Once Carolyn arrived home, introductions were made and we soon elected to eat at a local restaurant. At dinner we discussed the health care crisis for four hours. Over steaming-hot plates of pasta, we took turns describing our various experiences in the health care profession. I explained that my reason for the trip was to participate in a planning session, specifically to organize a retreat for hospital board members to learn about the concept of wellness and complementary medicine. Carolyn expressed a very strong interest in our efforts. As a nurse, she had firsthand experience with the limitations of Western medicine.

That night, as I headed to the bathroom to brush my teeth, I again passed by the wall of family photographs. Carolyn met me in the hall and through the photographs introduced her family to me: her husband, Tony, and her two grown children, Jerry and Lori. During the night, asleep on the living room couch, I had a dream. In the dream I walked into the kitchen to get a glass of water. Standing by the refrigerator was a tall man, about thirty-two years old with long brown hair, brown eyes, and a ruggedly handsome face. He introduced himself to me as Larry and said he was Carolyn's son. He asked me to give her a message, that he "was all right, everything was all right—not to worry." I agreed to relay the message.

The next morning, I awoke to hear Carolyn making breakfast. I got up and walked into the kitchen, at which point I suddenly remembered the dream, which I then shared with her. I added, "It's funny, he doesn't look anything like his photograph on the wall." Carolyn's eyes grew wide. She took a deep breath and then gave me a broad smile. "There is no way you could have ever known this. Larry was my first son. He died of Sudden Infant Death Syndrome at the age of six months. He did have dark hair and brown eyes and he would be about thirty years old, had he lived. His birthday was last week and I was wondering about him." Then she added, "I guess I had shut myself off from him, and now he communicated through you to speak to me."

I sat down and drew a big sigh, rubbing the goose bumps on my arms.

For the rest of my visit I noticed a slight but welcome change in Carolyn. She walked with confidence. I have seen this before in others. Hope realized will do that.

> If the wind in your sails can only bring you to the shores of hope, hoist your anchor and go. But keep your eyes set on the horizon of faith. It is there, and, in time, it will appear.

P.S. In early summer 1997, Carolyn's husband, Tony, died quite suddenly of pancreatic cancer. It was a tragic loss for Carolyn, as well as her two children. Shortly thereafter, a wonderful ceremony was held to honor the man she loved. As Tony's ashes were scattered to the four winds, Carolyn turned to her daughter, Lori, and, thinking of the dream I shared with her about her first son Larry, she then looked up at the sky and yelled, "Damn it, Tony, don't wait thirty years to tell me you're alright—give me a sign right now!" Within moments, the most gorgeous rainbow appeared on the horizon.

Stressed Is Desserts Spelled Backward

Mountains, molehills, and days from hell,
A world with too much change,
But I will make it, I know I will,
All it takes is a seed of faith.
How does that expression go?
Stressed is desserts spelled backward.

Cancer, loss, and the fear of death,
Those dark nights of the soul,
But the alchemy of love is pure,
Lead always turns to gold,
This much I know, this is true,
Stressed is desserts spelled backward.

Blessings, gifts, and silver clouds,
and lemonade galore,
It's humor, hope, faith, and love,
That get us through the storm,
Looking back, it's very clear,
Stressed is desserts spelled backward.

Resource Guide

Organizations

Bio-Relax
Mietek Wirkus
4803 St. Elmo Avenue
Bethesda, MD 20814
(301) 652-1691

Boulder Institute for Nature and the Human Spirit
Elizabeth Roberts
1314 8th Street
Boulder, CO 80302
(303) 939-8398

The Herb Research Foundation
107 Pearl Street
Boulder, CO 80301
(303) 449-2265

The Humor Project
Joel Goodman
480 Broadway, Suite 210
Sarasota Springs, NY
12866-2230
(518) 587-8770

Inspiration Unlimited
Brian Luke Seaward, Ph.D.
P.O. Box 18831
Boulder, CO 80308
(303) 678-9962

Institute of Noetic Sciences
475 Gate Five Road,
Suite 300
Sausalito, CA 94965
(415) 331-5650

International Society for the Study of Subtle Energy and Energy Medicine (ISSSEEM)
Golden, CO 80403-1347
(303) 425-4625

National Wellness Institute
National Wellness
Conference
P.O. Box 827
Stevens Point, Wisconsin
54481-0827
(800) 243-8694

Team Building and Laughter
Donna Strickland, M.S., R.N.
P.O. Box 100548
Denver, CO 80250
(303) 777-7997

Trees for Life
Balbir Mathur
3006 W. St. Louis
Wichita, KS 67203-5129
(316) 945-0629

TuneTown Records
Greg Tamblyn
P.O. Box 45258
Kansas City, MO 64111
(816) 757-7250

Recommended Reading

Robert Becker. *Cross Currents.* Los Angeles: Jeremy P. Tarcher, Inc., 1990.

Russell Blaylock. *Exitotoxins: The Taste that Kills.* Santa Fe, NM: Health Press, 1994.

Patrick Carnes. *Out of the Shadows.* Center City, NM: Hazelden Publishing, 1992.

Nick Del Calzo. *The Triumphant Spirit.* Denver, CO: Triumphant Spirit Publishing,1997.

Larry Dossey. *Healing Words.* San Francisco: HarperSanFrancisco. 1994.

Gerald Epstein. *Healing Visualizations.* New York: Bantam Books. 1989.

Richard Gerber. *Vibrational Medicine.* Santa Fe, NM: Bear & Co., 1988.

Allen Klein. *The Healing Power of Humor.* New York: Tarcher Books, 1989.

Elizabeth Kübler-Ross. *Death Does Not Exist.* Berkeley, CA: Celestial Arts Press, 1991.

Harriet Lerner. *The Dance of Anger.* New York: Perennial Press, 1985.

Patricia Norris and Garret Porter. *Why Me? Harnessing the Healing Power of the Human Spirit.* Walpole, NH: Stillpoint Press, 1985.

Elizabeth Roberts and Elias Amidon, editors. ***Earth Prayers.*** New York: HarperCollins, 1991.

______. ***Prayers For 1,000 Years.*** New York: HarperCollins, 1999.

Brian Luke Seaward. ***Stand Like Mountain, Flow Like Water: Reflections on Stress and Human Spirituality.*** Deerfield Beach, FL: Health Communications, Inc., 1987.

Claire Sylvia. ***A Change of Heart.*** New York: Little Brown, 1997.

Words of Gratitude

As a child, my mother would read me stories, fairy-tales, fables, and real-life adventures—always with a message or moral at the end. I am ever so grateful to her and to her spirit, which lives on in this tradition. My deepest and most sincere thanks to my agent Tom Grady, who, quite literally, is a prayer answered. I also wish to thank the staff of Conari Press, particularly Mary Jane Ryan, who is a master at nurturing creative writing talents, as well as Claudia Schaab, Nancy Margolis, Brenda Knight, Robin Demers, Sharon Donovan, and Will Glennon for all your efforts—thanks for giving this book a great home!

Once again, I wish to express special thanks to my personal assistant, Susan Griffin, who is always an inspiration. Heartfelt thanks also to Skylar, Mary Jane, Dan, Laurie C. B., Bonnie, Nuell P., and Mary Linda, who gave me some great feedback along the way, as well as the many friends who supported my budding career as an author—you know who you are!

My humble gratitude and best wishes to Joan Lunden for a wonderful Foreword; I am deeply indebted to your kindness. Thanks for giving this book your special blessing. A gracious thank-you to my colleagues Deepak Chopra, Naomi Judd, Richard Carlson, and Dave Scott, for their words of praise on the back cover. Thanks as well to Peter Alexander, for kind permission to adapt the *hogan* prayer story from his collection *Spiritual Archives*.

Most of all, I would like to thank all those people who shared their stories with me and invited me to be a part of their lives: Andreí K., Dan P., Sandi L., John P., Joan C., Donna S., Robert S., Andrew A., Naomi J., Rabia R., Pat N., Pedro E., Betty S., J. P., Gail W., Joanne H., Balbir M., Darren D., Carolyn Z., Katy T., Pete K., Sheila S., Greg T., George S., Gladys M., Allison F., Robert S., Randy V., Eric S., and Michael P.

Last but not least, I offer my humble gratitude to the Source of all Creation, who blesses my life in every way. Thanks for the gentle winds of grace.

Bon Appetit!

About the Author

Brian Luke Seaward, Ph.D., is a faculty member of the University of Colorado, Boulder, and adjunct professor at the University of Northern Colorado, Greeley, Colorado. He is the executive director of Inspiration Unlimited, a health promotion consulting firm in Boulder, Colorado. Dr. Seaward is the author of *Stand Like Mountain, Flow Like Water: Reflections on Stress and Human Spirituality* and *Managing Stress; A Creative Journal.*

Throughout his career, Dr. Seaward has cultivated and mastered profound expertise in the areas of stress management, mind-body-spirit healing, and human spirituality. His accomplishments and insights in these areas, as well as in other aspects of the study of human consciousness, have earned him accolades at academic institutions, national and international conferences, workshops, and seminars. Brian Luke Seaward has earned an international reputation as an accomplished teacher, consultant, lecturer, author, and mentor.